LITERACY OF THE OTHER

SUNY series, Transforming Subjects: Psychoanalysis, Culture, and Studies in Education

Deborah P. Britzman, editor

LITERACY OF THE OTHER

RENARRATING HUMANITY

Aparna Mishra Tarc

SUNY
PRESS

Published by State University of New York Press, Albany

Printed in the United States of America

For information, contact State University of New York Press, Albany, NY
www.sunypress.edu

Production, Jenn Bennett
Marketing, Michael Campochiaro

Library of Congress Cataloging-in-Publication Data

Mishra Tarc, Aparna, 1969–
Literacy of the other : renarrating humanity / Aparna Mishra Tarc.
pages cm. — (SUNY series, transforming subjects : psychoanalysis, culture, and studies in education)
Includes bibliographical references and index.
ISBN 978-1-4384-5747-5 (hardcover : alk. paper)
ISBN 978-1-4384-5749-9 (e-book)
1. Reading, Psychology of. 2. Literacy—Psychological aspects. 3. Literacy—Study and teaching. 4. Humanism in literature. I. Title.

BF456.R2M57 2015
302.2'244—dc23 2014038019

10 9 8 7 6 5 4 3 2 1

Contents

Acknowledgments

This book has been writing itself from the earliest days of my childhood. At a tender age, my incredibly creative parents gifted me with a storied existence. Real and fictional stories filled my childhood in conversations at my mom's dinner table, in my dad's weekly public library excursions and in my invented worlds in the backyard with my siblings, Bob Mishra and Krissy Carrington. I am grateful to my fabulous, loving, and delightfully flawed family for giving me such a vibrant and heartfelt world of stories with which to become someone. A life lived in story is a gift that I pass on to my children and students.

My work is indebted to the thought and support of my mentor and dear colleague Deborah Britzman. In her many books, Professor Britzman opened my mind to the infinite, creative possibility of freedom of the inner world. Her teaching gifted me with a magical, incisive vocabulary that brings form and meaning to my faltering phrase. And although these words are mine, this book, Deborah, is written with our conversations in mind.

Children and students inspire and press me to think, teach, and write in service of others. Although there are too many to mention here, I wish to acknowledge my brief time with one student, Abshir Hassan, a brilliant, gentle, and kind person whose life was taken too quickly and violently at the merciless hands of another. The final pages of this book contain a trace of my grief at the thought of the world bereft of you, Abshir. Our encounter was too brief yet profound. Your words and memory will influence our shared struggle and commitment to do justice to the unique potential of each student in our classrooms and in schools and in the worlds beyond both.

My colleagues and friends at York University continue to shape and support my intellectual and emotional life. In particular I give thanks to Steve Alsop, Chloe Brushwood-Rose, Roopa Desai-Trilokekar, Susan Dion, Rishma Dunlop, Troy Fraser, Esther Fine, Jen Gilbert,

John Ippolito, David Lewkovich, Celia Haig-Brown, Didi Khayatt, Naomi Norquay, Lyndon Martin, Alice Pitt, Kim Tavares, Diane Vetter, Sue Winton, and the late Patrick Solomon, who believed in me from the minute we first met.

Smaro Kamboureli recognized something compelling about my work when I was a doctoral student, and so unsure and unsteady with my thought. Raw versions of this book were presented at three conferences hosted by Professor Kamboureli's TransCanada Literary Institute. In many ways this book was written in dialogue with many talented colleagues in attendance at these scholarly venues. Thank you so much Smaro for including me in this incredible bounty of thought and creation, and for bringing attention to the important work of Canadian literary writers, poets, critics, and emerging scholars in the national and international scene.

As important as the chance to publicly present this work at the Institute is the generative response of my brilliant, literary colleagues. For their ongoing provocation of literary ideas, I am grateful to Phanuel Antwi, Diana Brydon, Christian Bök, Richard Cassidy, David Chariandy, Lily Cho, Amber Dean, Jill Didur, Kit Dobson, Angela Facundo, Jade Ferguson, Len Findlay, Terry Goldie, Jennifer Henderson, Nat Hurley, Mark Lipton, Ashok Mathur, Roy Miki, Sophie McCall, Mark McCutcheon, Elan Paulson, Donna Penne, Julie Rak, Stephen Slemon, Pauline Wakeham, and the late Barbara Godard.

For his contribution to my literary ideas and his hospitable reception of my work, I am grateful to Daniel Coleman. Professor Coleman's acute and sublime thought of the co-existential significance of an examined and meditative literary life resonates so deeply in mine. I continue to learn from his books that travel through inside lives and across social difference.

Tracy Chapman, J. M. Coetzee, Jacques Derrida, Carolyn Forché, Toni Morrison, and Bruce Springsteen teach me that one does not have to know someone to be greatly affected by their words, service, and existence. I continue to learn how to read, write, and live from these writers of infinite and possible humanity. Their words pull me through the best and darkest of times.

Close friendship is the most critical element of intellectual work. I thank Lisa Farley for holding constantly the more difficult aspects of my thinking, RM Kennedy for his sensitive, erudite, and loving insight, David Errington for his courage and fight in an unfair world, Daniel Yon for reminding me that some reservation in communication is necessary, Mario Di Paolantonio for demonstrating the fiercest of thought is also gentle, Don Dippo for his insistence of justice through service, Judith Robertson for her sense of beauty and priority for all living things that deserve love and attention, Sarah Twomey for her world of adventure and love of small things, Debbi Sonu, for her gift of dance, Julie Bryd-Clarke and Steve Clarke for their infectious love of story, Andre Carrington for his musical voice, Colin Couchman for his thoughts on books and film and for his care of my family, Kent den Heyer for the laughter, Nicholas Ng-Fook for his open invitation to wonder, Rubén Gaztambide-Fernández for lifting my thought, Jen Blair for lifting my spirit, and Warren Crichlow for his exquisite notes on the pressing matter of living in the world with others. I am always grateful to Andy and Betty Tarc and to Glenn and Shirley Eastabrook, who are teachers and second parents to Paul Tarc and me.

I greatly appreciate the support of Beth Bouloukos, Jenn Bennett, and the editorial staff at SUNY Press, throughout the publication process. First books are precious objects and I thank the editors and anonymous reviewers for the close attention and care they have taken with my thought and writing. I also thank Deborah Britzman for supporting this work for publication in the SUNY series: *Transforming subjects: Psychoanalysis, culture, and studies in education.*

I thank both Sage Publications (www.sagepub.com) and Taylor and Francis Publications (www.tandfonline.com) for their permission to draw from earlier versions of this work. Parts of chapter 1 were originally published as "Literacy of the Other: The Inner Life of Literacy," in the *Journal of Early Childhood Literacy*. An earlier version of chapter 4 was originally published as "Disturbing Reading. J. M. Coetzee's 'The Problem of Evil,'" in the journal *Changing English*. I wish to give a special mention to Jane Miller, chief editor of *Changing English* for her much-needed and generous support of young scholars with innovative approaches to literacy, literary thought, and literature.

I am thankful for the support of my many academic colleagues at home and in the world: Vanessa Andreotti, Nina Asher, Tamara Bibby, Kate Cairns, Sara Childer, Roland Sintos Coloma, Stephanie Daza, Kari Dehli, Lynn Mario De Souza, Jane Kenway, Carl Leggo, Magda Lewis, Jeong-Eun Rhee, Fazal Rizvi, Lisa Taylor, Ricky Varghese, and Lisa Weems. Their enthusiastic reception of my work and mind makes me brave. I also thank Stephanie Springgay and Debra Freedman for their commitment to scholarship on and by (m)others. As well I thank all my colleagues at the Postcolonial SIG at AERA and the Canadian Association of Curriculum Studies for continuing to support my thinking. I acknowledge the Social Science and Humanities Council of Canada for funding various presentations of my work and for supporting the publication of early versions of this work.

Even with a brilliant intellect and voracious passion for reading, my father, Anu Mishra, would see his mind, memory, and desire tested in the twilight of his life with the onset of dementia. In this time of great anguish, consoling us all, are stories of his mother, mother tongue, motherland retold by my beautiful, inventive, and caregiving mother, Chhaya Mishra. These days his unthinkable experience brings home the significance of literacy situated in an immigrant's childhood. It is his maternal experience of language in the earliest moments of his life and his adult life with my mother that comfort and compel him now to keep living, with quality and meaning, despite or in spite of facing the cruelest of mentally lived conditions. Now as ever, in their struggle to coexist and survive the fantastic and existential ravages of lost memory, my parents urge me to read, write, love, and live as if every single person's life depended on it. Now as ever I am reminded of the great existential significance of literacy of the Other in the bittersweet family story of our lives.

Among all, I profoundly thank Paul Tarc, my first and faithful reader, for his quiet companionship, generous mind, and incredible capacity for care, and for carrying so painstakingly my faltering thoughts and fragile feeling in his heart. From you and our four beautiful children, Gabi, Ana, Rebecca, and James, I am gifted with a story of meaningful existence of love, struggle, acceptance, and reparation. A thought of you, Paul, is in every word I write. You mean every*thing* to me.

I dedicate this book to the late Dr. Roger I. Simon whom I met in words in his first book. You changed my life for good, Roger. Our face-to-face encounters in memory, in writing, and in mind *sustain* me.

Introduction

Literacy of the Other

> You must write, and read, as if your life depended upon it. That is not generally taught in school.
>
> —Adrienne Rich, *What Is Found There*

I first came across Adrienne Rich's imperative to write and reac if one's life depended on it" in my English literature undergrac degree. I stumbled onto her sentence in an English class engagin erary works written by minority populations: women, African Aı cans, postcolonial writers. Literary encounters with these fictional brought me strangely home. As fictional characters struggled to front colonial discourses that demeaned their lives, I was transf back to my childhood. There I met with memories of my first f ing attempts to speak of an inner existence maligned and liberat language. Without words to describe my fraught relation to the E language, I was stunned by feelings of devastation, repair, and cı renewal animated by the affective force of a single sentence.

This book's argument is simple: language indelibly affects u survival and the quality of our existence depend on language to and live. This book's central position hinges on Rich's insight eracy: survival of ourselves depends on how we enter into aı language. I define literacy as our lifelong initiations into and co with various idioms, structures, forms, dialects, and cadences guage. Language and our use of it can potentially and violently c various forms of sentient life. Novel uses of language can also cr

renew and shape the formation that our selves might take. Language makes us suffer and want to live.

Half a lifetime passed for me to understand the significance of Rich's insight stirring up faint memories of the rough linguistic terrain of an immigrant girl's childhood. My first sense of the existential significance of language is as a first-generation Canadian girl, raised by immigrant South Asian parents in a small city in Ontario. Growing up in the early seventies after the civil rights movements was difficult for immigrant children. When my older brother returned home on the first day of kindergarten devastated by his teacher's failure to understand him, the Canadian government's policy of linguistic and cultural assimilation, educationally sanctioned at the time, was enacted in the privacy of our household. To ensure some belonging to Canadian culture and life, my father forbade his children to speak our native tongue, Bengali.

As the first child of one fully and one barely bilingual parent, my brother's early literacy consisted of a faltering spoken English littered with Bengali phrases. Terror at the abject reception of his child by school officials prompted my father into a hyper-defensive stance against his mother tongue. His decision was designed to protect his children from unforeseen dangers when participating in English Canadian public life. Much to my mother's dismay, my father declared on that day, his children would learn to read and write only in English. Not only would we learn English: we would learn to read and write above and beyond the capacity of native speakers. We would learn to read and write English because our lives depended on it.

As the second-born child, at the tender age of three, I was denied access to my mother tongue except in secret moments of mother-child relation. I recall little but I do remember taking in some of my mother's sorrow with the silencing of our mother tongue in our home. This sorrow remains inside my words to this day. But losing the mother tongue had another curious side effect: I became a precocious English speaker delighting in every turn of phrase and new expression I learned. "Your daughter talks too much," my teachers declared to the utter chagrin of my severely reserved father. And indeed, I was vocally compulsive. Driven by a need for communication, I inhaled and expelled words like air. I hung on to each newly acquired turn of phrase like a lifeboat. And despite my growing proficiency in English, I kept company and a secret kinship with my mother tongue. In those three initial years of Bengali immersion I built an incredible capacity to understand my

mother's language, without ever developing a capacity for fluency and formal comprehension. Somehow my inner life and interpretive capacity became conditioned by my mother tongue. Maybe I absorbed a second language cadence through the comfort of my parents' late night conversations. Or perhaps Bengali became insinuated in me through inside recitations of their language I performed over and over again. Immersed in these invented rituals of psychical literacy, I taught myself to become well versed in a silenced litany of origins lost yet reinvented somewhere in the torn fabric of immigrant life. In this practice of affectively taking in an unknown yet familiar language, I internalized my parents' broken-English structure of sorrow and struggle for the loss of their homeland and their hopes for promise of a new land. I can see their cross-cultural conflicts reflected in my more experimental and intuitive practices of English.

As my father hoped I became fairly adept with English. My relation with English grew more complicated as I became a lifelong reader, teacher, scholar, and writer of English. As my relations with language unfolded, literacy opened doors for a young foreigner struggling to navigate two vastly different worlds. I longed to be Canadian despite having little cultural capital and community ties; I was also consumed with saving something of the prior affective mother tongue traced in my excessive uses and abuses of English. I am reminded of this existential crisis in my idiomatic and wild use of language, when I wage words with passionate exuberance, when I am told that my words do not make sense and when I am confronted with difficulty and the world seems to overwhelm.

My story shares resemblances with anyone learning a new language. Even though unique circumstances heightened my understanding of the link between language and existence, at an early age most children realize that language is key to their survival. Understated in most formal schooling is the extent to which language acquisition and production provide the conditions for the child to experience acknowledgment of her lived realities and a meaningful and healthy quality of living. Kelly Oliver stresses this profound and yet incredibly understated dimension of literacy:

> We are all born into a world in which meaning already exists and is not our own. Yet we make it our own by using language and learning to communicate as a form of communion. What happens, however, when within the language

> and culture into which we are born, within the dominant culture, we exist as other, subhuman, animals, slaves, or denigrated beings? How can we make this language and meaning our own? What are the consequences of owning a meaning that disowns you in your very being, in your very body? How can bodily drives and affects make their way into language if that language articulates that body and its affects as abject? Without loving social support, without the loving third,[1] making meaning one's own and thereby experiencing life and language as meaningful becomes complicated, if not perverse and self-destructive. (Oliver 2002, 55–56)

Oliver suggests that the quality of one's life is marked by dominant and private uses of language. Demeaning uses of language can vastly influence the existence of a person. Meaningful and expressive forms of language can support the full potential of a living thing. Having been subject to both forms of language as a member of a minority and dominant group, I have learned that the use of language for and against someone matters. Meaningful and expressive uses of language have benefited me in ways that my father never imagined. A heightened, interior, and deeply reverent orientation toward words and sentences supports me to participate fully and powerfully in my public life as a teacher and a scholar. Still, my immigrant experience supports me to understand that there are grave consequences to being made abject through forms of language meant to demean and injure the other's humanity. Not only do dehumanizing forms of language demean others from the inside out, but these forms of discourse also diminish the possible meanings we might create for social life and our humanity. According to Derrida, there are grave, secondary social effects for failing to acknowledge the first and "originary" violence of language, a violence that consists "in inscribing within a difference, in classifying, in suspending the vocative absolute" (1976a, 112). He warns that the generative possibilities of language can be diminished by an overreliance on instrumental, systematic, and classifying practices of literacy. His work (1978b), like mine, demonstrates an expressed commitment to excavating and constructing literacies that gives way to generative possibilities, experimentation, and play in our understandings and uses of language.

In this book, I explore the inner life of literacy in fictional conceptions of human life. Acknowledging the existential effects of literacy I argue that inventive language has the capacity to creatively address forms of life that the "humanizing" discourses routinely dismiss (Lyotard 1991). Along with taking a leading role in mental development, I suggest that literacy supports a humanizing process with an accompanying narrative of transformation from inhuman to human states. The global spread of modern life is through English literacy, giving rise to the critical role of linguistic forms in fashioning human thought and existence. The paradox of literacy is that language can both renew and diminish the lives of others. My intervention does not theorize a new way of "doing literacy" although I do hope that some of the conceptualization put forth in this book affects existing theories and practices of literacy. Neither is this a book an attack on literacy, as its central tenet advances the idea that we need common, intelligible, and *humane* structures of language by which to live. Instead, I put into question dominant forms and contents of the human story garnered through normative assumptions informing the psychosocial practice of literacy. I provide teachers and scholars a means to think about literacy in any language as inherent to the philosophical and cultural construction of humanizing narratives of existence and to the possibility of renewing those existential narratives. It can be difficult to think of literacy once one is literate, so I use literature to gain some perspective on how language forms and informs thought. Turning to literature, I think literacy beyond its instrumental conception as learning to decode and decipher symbolic print and also beyond its naturalized association with English.

To be made recognizable to others, children must express their need in intelligible form to another who lovingly accepts and carefully returns their faltering symbolic constructions. Literacy, in this book, also refers to the sticky cointerpretive frames and inherited forms of reference that we acquire from the mother in infancy to make meaning of people and things as we learn to use a language and subsequent languages. Literacy in this conception includes the relational pedagogical means by which we learn to use, abuse, and renew the dominant forms of language we depend on to recognize, interpret, and represent our existence and those of others in our midst.

In *Monolingualism of the Other*, Jacques Derrida (1998) eloquently constructs a significant aspect of the theory of literacy this book advances. Monolingualism is Derrida's metaphor for internalized literacy. Literacy provides us with the intelligible communicative structure, or "logos," giving form to thinking and articulation to our thoughts.

Every language has a dominant linguistic structure and common usage by which that language is made intelligible to members of its society. No language is exempt from a structure of intelligibility, although logos is not fixed and is mutable; it is plastic and manipulated by users as they pass through a social and cultural context (Derrida 1976a). Old English and texting English are examples of the way the structure of a language radically mutates and evolves through social usage and technological advance. The important point here is not about a particular linguistic structure but the need for there to exist a common order to discourse in a society to which the child is subjected as a condition of her gaining membership to the adult community.

With the idea that we learn to articulate ourselves through monolingualism of the Other, Derrida reminds us that we are bound to the other's structure of language, worn-down meanings, and common sense. For Derrida, no language is our own. At birth, our mother tongue, the other's tongue, overwrites us from the inside out: our unique sense of self is lost as the originary interior childhood existence is conscripted to the language and the culture of our birthright. The rights of man afforded to us through symbolic law exceed personal attachments to the mother tongue. The idea that one has natural rights to any given language is a cruel but necessary illusion. Language is not fixed to a time or space but is mutable and perpetually evolving and changing, and so does not belong to a single person or cultural community. Paradoxically, Derrida insists: "Yes, I only have one language, yet it is not mine" (Derrida 1998, 2).

Derrida did not come to his theory of language solely through the sophisticated framework of grammatology or the poststructural linguistic theory of deconstruction; he stumbled onto his claim that "nothing exists without text" through an existential narrative that bears striking resemblance to my own. Derrida's ideas of language enter the scene at early childhood in school. As the profoundly sensitive son of Jewish Algerian immigrants, the child Derrida would devastatingly encounter the formal requirement to learn the proper norming language of school. Derrida recounts his inner, boyhood pain as "a little black and very Arab Jew" stumbling to exist in his French Algerian *lycée* with a fledgling command of the French language and a marginalized religious and ethnic affiliation (in Peeters 2012, 19). The loss of his Sephardic Jewish mother's tongue by the *lycée*'s injunction that he learn to speak "proper" French has a strange effect on the child "'Jackie" Derrida: his linguistic and cultural loss makes him want to learn and be French better than a Frenchman (in Peeters 2012). For better and worse, French becomes the way for Derrida (1998), the child, to find, speak, and name his thoughts of himself, others, and the world.

A lifetime passed before he penned a highly acclaimed meditation on the lasting pedagogical effects of a wounding language initiation. Derrida theorizes language as both alienating and affirming the child's unique sense of her self. He finds that language, the singular mode and method by which one is given to the mother's tongue determine what one can make and is made of oneself.

> We only ever speak one language—and, since it returns to the other, it exists asymmetrically, always for *the other*, from the other, kept by the other. Coming from the other, remaining with the other, and returning to the other. (1998, 40)

In this memoir of language development spanning a lifetime, Derrida poignantly writes of the impossibility of creating a narrative of one's own when those narratives are always given to one by the other.[2] The other's language is also not hers alone steeped in the language of a society and culture. Affirming that language is idiosyncratically comprised of one's unique idiom, the fleeting trace of one's internal world, Derrida reminds us that socially determined narratives of human existence overwrite our internal sense of our self. We are mapped as "healthy," "boy," "girl," and given a proper name before we have recourse to protest that our insides fail to match up to any of those determinations. As we grow, we might learn other names that describe our externalized realities based on evident markers: sex organs, skin color, body size, and physical appearance. We learn that some names given to us by others do not feel like us. Names might hurt us more than sticks and stones, as it can take a lifetime to purge from internal recesses of the mind and body the trauma of another's literacy that demeans our unique existence. We can also learn to delight in language given to us by the other as we begin to name others outside our self to know them. We can feel appreciative that language expresses our kind. With growing familiarity with the other's words, we learn of things we can destroy and create through a single word.

One's earliest relation with language forcibly orients one's sexual and sensational body into a world of meaning already made up of social ties, bonds, and contracts. Language gives one lessons on how to be human in a body driven by erotic, sentient impulses. Yet this fundamental, prelinguistic stage of person development is foreclosed by philosophical, critical, and educational theories of the mind and body.

Most cognitive theories of literacy mark the child's entry into language, and thus thinking, with the spoken word. Speaking provides the self with evidence that he or she is an "I," a self-creating-self, a thinking subject in charge of her thoughts. Derrida insists an overdependence on the spoken word also fools the adult community into believing that the child does not "think" before the moment of intelligible articulation.

> If hearing-oneself-speak, in so far as it also passes through a certain mouth, transforms everything into auto-affection, assimilates everything to itself by idealizing it within interiority, masters everything by mourning its passing, refusing to touch it, to digest it naturally, but digests it ideally, consumes what it does not consume and *vice versa,* produces disinterestedness in the possibility of pronouncing judgments . . . what is the border or the absolute overboard [*le bord ou le débord absolu*] of this problematic? (Derrida 1981, 20)

Speech, as the external evidence of truth of the self, is misleading. Falling in love with our voice we idealize speech as evidence of a higher capacity to think for ourselves. Speaking, Derrida suggests, rides on this primary narcissism, an autoaffection that can delude the self into actively forgetting that one's capacity to speak is not of the self but of the (m)other. Pointing to primary structures of dependence, Derrida argues that language is given to us by our (m)other at birth. For this reason Derrida claims: "1. We only ever speak one language. 2. We never speak only one language" (Derrida 1998, 7). In our mind, the mother's tongue coheres with our internal sense of the world. This coherence produces an inner writing that informs and forms symbolic communication. Our thoughts are already forming in the other's words as we speak our own. Words spoken by the self betray a trace of the other.

For Derrida, writing does not refer to the one-to-one correspondence of speech to the word or word to print. Writing corresponds to the mind's "imprint" articulating a spoken or printed symbol (Derrida 1976a). We learn to 'write' our sense of the world and others before we utter a single sound. Cognition and thinking is an effect of the internalized symbolic interpretive register *relationally* given to us in our infancy by a (m)other. We depend on this internal register to think, speak, and communicate ourselves in relation and with judgment to others and the world. On forms of social communication, we transfer an imperceptible psychical imprint of our infantile communication with (m)other. After Derrida, we might view literacy as operating pedagogically, as a maternal imprint steering our lifelong capacities to express ourselves through symbolic communication.

Literacy begins to colonize the child's inside lives as she begins to express her self. As Derrida vividly depicts, the scene of literacy is one that forcibly and irretrievably removes the child from the maternal relation.

> Writing—already in the tongue—would operate, with regard to immediate adherence, somewhat like the red-eyed father who shames the young ape, like "his gaze which, like fire, unhooks the child from the mother, unhooks the mother from the child, the child that has become her tree" (Abraham, *L'instinct filial*, 14). (Derrida 1976b, 9)

Derrida qualifies this Oedipal scene as one infused with eros and violence, one further described by his English-language translator Peggy Kamuf as "reinflict[ing] the violence that wrenches the human animal out of the state of sheer animality" (Kamuf 2000, 12). Derrida's depiction of the ordinary violence accompanying the primal scene of language learning characterizes the pedagogical or relational means by which the child is forced into language. As the young child attempts to nakedly communicate she is abruptly ripped from maternal embodied expressions of existence and silently sealed in the paternal law of language. Through these primary scenes of alienation and shame, the child is rid of her animal self and, by association, her animal mother. The process of forcing the animate existence in a container of symbols pedagogically initiates and later colonizes her unique self into the normative restraints of culture.

In his essay "About the Human," Jean Francois Lyotard argues that to become literate in any human language is to become removed from one's first in-human nature.

> Shorn of speech, incapable of standing upright, hesitating over the objects of its interest, not able to calculate its advantages, not sensitive to common reason, the child is

> eminently the human because its distress heralds and promises things possible. Its initial delay in humanity, which makes it the hostage of the adult community, is also what manifests to this community the lack of humanity it is suffering from, and which calls on it to become more human. (Lyotard 1991, 3–4)

The dependent infant animates terror in the adult community who sees the little animal thing in desperate need of human form. Language generates the cultural forms by which the child is worded and, with the word, disciplined into the human community. Language forcibly humanizes us according to particular forms of logos and cultural norms. However, Lyotard argues that this humanizing education tends to use dehumanizing processes to rush the baby into human form. Rushing the child to language we also rush the child out of her primary animal being. We contain her sentient existence in words. Still, if the infant is behaviorally rid of her animal existence, it remains stirring inside the words used to silence its rumblings. Madeline Grumet (1988) suggests that these first pedagogical scenes of language learning are not only cognitively significant; these first efforts at learning a first and subsequent language are also Oedipal and infused with misrecognition, shame, domination, and longing at the hands of the other. Language is an existential as well as a cognitive and symbolic consequence of the infant child being born to those already socialized into a variant of human being. A fraught infantile beginning compels the baby's need for language and subsequent human formation.

Literacy, then, is implicated in systematizing thought and being. Literacy radically determines the human limits and possibilities for thinking and communicating with others. Literacy as one's initiation into social life teaches the child the rule of language. She must follow these internalized rules of a common language to make her body recognizable to others. These rules assimilate the child's unique inner processes for thinking within dominant and accepted symbolic forms. Yet literacy also provides the necessary means to critique and potentially alter the governing forms of life language creates. Following Derrida, Gayatri Spivak refers to literacy as a *pharmakon* or curing substance, which, when used in a certain way, can help or harm us.

> Literacy is poison as well as medicine. It allows us to sense that the other is not just a "voice"—others also produce

> articulated texts, even as they, like us, are written in and by a text not of our own making. (Spivak 1997, 483)

For Spivak, literacy both helps and harms the human animal. Literacy teaches us to make and express our thoughts but it also teaches us to privilege Thought. Grounded in logos, conventional literacy teaches us to presence the Self over all "Others" and to privilege reason over emotion. Reorienting literacy in our felt response to others can serve to alter dominant forms and usages of language that diminish sentient life.

The role of literacy in securing a particular kind of human existence is a less examined aspect of its operation, although indigenous and postcolonial theorists have understood the power of English language and literacy in colonizing projects of human oppression (Freire 1982; Giroux 1990; Willinsky 1998). Compulsory literacy of the colonizer's language seems to monstrously repeat the primary alienation the child experiences from her sentient existence. To highlight the brutal effects of a dehumanizing literacy, indigenous and colonial populations cite cultural genocide as a direct effect of the devastating and often irreparable loss of native and mother tongue. Postcolonial scholars also recognize that literacy can be put to use to determine the worth or unworthiness of a life according to particular mindsets and measures (Derrida 1986; Spivak 1999). The global movement of English, for example, is tied to an economic system and technological advances that form human minds and bodies according to a capitalist, consumerist ideology. However, that movement of English has other unintended effects. English might support increased communication and cooperation across national boundaries as well. If the French colonized the French Algerian Derrida into being more "correctly" French than a Frenchman, it also supports his capacity to use language to forge an incredible critique of Western ontology that exceeded mere cultural membership (in Attridge and Baldwin 2004).

Derrida's (1976a) playful, experimental, and imaginative use of the French language in the seminal work *Of Grammatology* gives rise to an incredible body of thought that liberated many from the constraints of normative discourse. My work insists that, although a necessary violence accompanies the child's social fall into language, a hospitable pedagogy of literacy might help soften the blow that the symbolic world wages on the child's unique sense of herself. This hospitable pedagogy might teach us to honor the other's language in the imposition of our own. Late modernist authors, such as those featured in this book, provide compelling examples of the role of colonizing language in the construction of fabulous theories of human diminishment and renewal, death and life, oppression and liberation. After colonialism, as our hypermodern use of language becomes reduced to sound bites and text messages, so might our incredible capacities for language and thinking continue to severely diminish. Urgent for the times we live is the idea that rich, deliberative, diverse, inventive, and meaningful forms and uses of language can support our capacity to narrate meaningful versions of human being and to build responsive and ethical relations with other sentient beings in this world we share.

Renarrating Humanity through Literature

In this book, I suggest that the psychosocial formation of literate subjects is storied. We internalize a felt capacity to unravel existential narratives communicated to us by our (m)others. The child's storied existence begins at birth when she is inserted into a world of others. In infancy we receive our first existential narratives upon receiving a normative determination of health and gender. Our story composed as personal is, in effect, based upon a universalized composition of the human. From these shaky normative narratives, we gain membership to a culturally bound society. Upon a sensate, sensual, and affective inner world bound to the care of mother, we learn to raggedly read the poetic fragments of the other's narrative that will come to define and determine our discursively mediated existence.

The stories we are told of ourselves by others mediate our relationship with language. If we are "hardwired for language," as Noam Chomsky (1975) suggests, others give us the internalized monolingual form and contents through which our first intelligible and audible sounds arrive. Even if we learn fluently to manipulate language we can still feel caught in the grips of linguistic difficulty when presented with ideas or people that do not quite fit with our narrative of being. Our relation to language is critical to our existence because it gives us the capacity to speak and write our lives.

Rereading literacy in this book, I examine the vexed relation between language learning and narratives of the human. In my inquiry I discuss four dimensions of rereading literacy, as follows: recasting literacy as fundamental to one's sense of the world and others; rethinking the potentialities of humanity that are effaced by becoming particularly literate; examining the context/conduct of patriarchal and European colonization in their centuries-long training of the human mind; and fostering pedagogies to support a literacy of the other toward renarrating humanity as dependent on the ontological narratives we offer our children to grant them membership to the social.

Literary depictions of literacy are the objects of this book. It can be hard to think of processes of literacy without distance from the mind. Literature affords us such distance. I analyze these depictions through the constructs and methods of child psychoanalyst Melanie Klein. I draw heavily on Klein's (1930) theory of symbolization to reconstruct the maternal scene of literacy. Klein suggests that the maternal scene writing the infant's internal sense of the world prepares the psychical grounds for a socializing literacy. Reorienting literacy to the maternal relation shifts the emphasis in literacy from observing how the child decodes words to observing how the child engages with and relates to worded stories of her self, others, and the world handed down to her by (m)other.[3] As I demonstrate in this book, a literacy of the Other considers the infant's formative relationships with narratives of existence told to her by (m)other. First reading is the placeholder for a person's lifelong story. The storied process by which the child becomes an active self is critical to her capacity to make meaningful relations between her self and others. Our humanity is created, destroyed, and renewed in the stories we tell to and of others. Narrative is a form of experimental psychosocial action that supports our capacity to act and be in relation to others and the world. Revising dominant narratives of humanity, as does some of the literature I discuss, alters the meanings of humanity and revitalizes the experience of being human.

To forge a rethinking of literacy as a return to its humanizing imperative, I turn to modern humanistic literature. Providing a juncture between the psychical and social worlds, literature gives indirect access to unconscious processes structuring human relations (Love 2007). Late modernist or "(post)colonial" literature, as are those works featured in this book, grapple with the more unthinkable aspect of human subject formation and relations. Because philosophical thinking has little addressed the inner life and the not known of knowledge, ontology offers a limited representation of the inside human condition. Particular engagements with literature offer human beings what other humanistic inquiry is unable to give—receptiveness to responding to the inside lives of Others (Coetzee 1999). Literature imagines and offers an ontic narrative of our inside life that we struggle to word using everyday parlance.

Literature also teaches us to enter into representation in less familiar ways. I attribute my generative and creative uses of English partly to my mother tongue and mostly to a life immersed in English literature. Literature is perhaps most adept at depicting the inner workings of the mind. Psychoanalysis recognizes this potential in and of literature. It is not by chance that Freud used literary works for his guide when naming libidinal processes; he found an inadequate vocabulary to image the mind's working in scientific and philosophical discourse (Lear 1999). Klein also used literary works to think through the more difficult aspects of her theories of internal life (Jacobus 1999). Adam Phillips (2000) has gone so far as to suggest that we reread psychoanalysis as a grand literary epic rather than a scientific treatise on the workings of the mind. Still, the novel invention, like Freud's incredible depiction of the psyche, has always been critical to the work of the human scientist and the human sciences.

My own approach to the psychoanalytic potential of the literary, notwithstanding existing debates, is that, as with literature, psychoanalysis offers an inventive vocabulary and allegorical structure with which to view the workings of the mind. Rather than read psychoanalysis as great literature per Adam Phillips's (2000) suggestion, I find form-defying evidence of psychoanalytic concepts embedded in the richly psychical processes of symbolization of the literary artist's craft. In fantastic depictions of real and fictional readers learning to grapple with the psychical effects of language as beginning readers, experienced readers, and violently colonized subjects, I find a basis for psychoanalytic constructs mapping out the internal and emotional world of literacy. E. R. Burroughs's *Tarzan* offers us a story of the enlightened and inhuman ape-boy who is humanized through a self-taught English literacy. The omnipotent version of literacy Burroughs presents arises from a dominant metaphysical fantasy of superior human dispositions projected onto the fictional figure of Tarzan, the ape-man. J. M. Coetzee's depiction of Elizabeth Costello, an unraveling reader fallen to infancy through a problem with reading, gives us insight into the dynamics of transference in reading. Coetzee's short story follows prior and repressed experiences of a reader as it compromises the interpretive apparatus with which she reads the world and others. Reading Toni Morrison's *Beloved* through Klein's theory of symbolic reparation, I demonstrate how Morrison models, in the aesthetic and formal operations of her text, a creative form of symbolic repair by which a community wracked by mass violence and social degradation might learn to again live. I call a person's or community's effort to symbolically renarrate, to renew dehumanizing linguistic and human forms, literacy of the Other, a literacy that seeks to do justice to the inner life, dreams, and lives of a person through the other's thoughtful and creative gift of words.

Novels offer scholars and teachers of literacy a glimpse of the inner lives of literacy by those who are most closely attuned to the inside workings of language—exemplary writers of literature. It is not simply enough for me to inform teachers that literature is useful in their pedagogy of literacy. I suggest that teachers prepare for their literacy pedagogy through sustained and trained readings of literature grappling with human existence. Literature can teach us of the unconscious yet deeply felt inner communions that take place in communicative encounter. Literature acknowledges interiority as it supports us to gain insight into the mysteries of the inner world. Literature attunes us to the emotional situation of language as it moves us to thinking.

My use of literature supports scholars and teachers of literacy to engage in psychoanalytic constructs through the depictions of fictional lives and events. By doing so I follow in the footsteps of the most innovative and daring of psychoanalytic and literary scholars (Britzman 2009a; Greene 1995; Grumet 1988; Jacobus 1999; Kristeva 2001; Love 2007; Spivak 1999; Rose 1984). Mary Jacobus gives instances where literature acts as the mirror of Klein's theory (Jacobus 1999, 11). Following Klein and other theorists (Derrida 1982; Britzman 2006b; Spivak 2002) who hold literature to theory's mirror, I hold literature to my "mirror"—literacy as language learning grounded in (infant) psychical development. Educators can gain greater insight into the human-making imperatives of literacy by examining representations of literacy in literature.

Two novelists featured in this book are Nobel Prize winners. All of the novels have been translated into multiple languages and read by millions of readers and/or turned into films. The literary works featured in this book are both global and exemplary. Because they are both exemplary and globally enjoyed, they are significant as literary artifacts and as a historical archive documenting the inner life of literate consciousness.

Outline of the Book

Each of the chapters in this study reconstructs the infant's or an infantile fall into language as critical to one's subject formation. Each chapter builds upon and illustrates my overarching argument that literacy is fundamental to each person's becoming. Chapter 1 grounds literacy in the maternal relation through Melanie Klein's object relations theory. This chapter explicates the book's main conception of literacy as marking the child's fall into language necessary to word her self and the world. I present literacy as a profoundly emotional situation where the act of symbolizing one's blurry and felt response to the world is of existential as well as intellectual significance. To pose literacy as an emotional situation, I give a case of my teaching experience of a child with problems in communication deemed to have behavioral problems. I turn to the work of Klein in search of a hospitable pedagogy of literacy that supports the inhibited child's efforts to symbolize a sense of her shaky insides to others. I suggest that a literacy that responds to the child's difficulty in expressing herself can support her to navigate the unfamiliar terrain of the social.

In chapter 2 I suggest that some literature foregrounds a more sophisticated process of the self's contention with language in the construction of real and fictional worlds. I demonstrate how some literature exemplifies a practice of literacy and a method for reading and writing the world that depends on one's infantile imaginative capacity to word one's self in relation to others. When we experience conflicts in literature we are reminded of an interpretive problem that is rooted in psychical literacy. Our learned frames of reference can interfere with our capacity to do justice to the other's life and the world in which we live. I link our interpretive capacity as adults to our first readings of the other and the world. These early readings are animated when we engage some literature, particularly those narratives that place our own in question. Analytic engagements with literature give us the opportunity to examine the desires we bring to our meanings of external reality that we are not allowed in real life encounters with others. This chapter also discusses the role that literature might play in the social sciences in developing a practice of micro reading of affections that circulate within our real accounts of the other and the world. The interpretive practice we gain through our engagements with literacy, as depicted in exemplary literature, can foster an altered relation to ourselves and to the other's lives.

In chapters 3 to 5, I turn briefly to three novels that give readers insight into four psychical processes at work in literacy: identification, projection, transference, and reparation. Using literary examples, I discuss the role that these processes play in one's understanding of literacy. In chapter 3, I examine how Tarzan learns to read and write. I attribute Burroughs's "rush" to secure Tarzan's literacy to the anxieties he displays toward animal and human "Others." These anxieties are projected on the figure of Tarzan and his fabulous yet foundational conception of literacy (Lyotard 1991). The reader's identification with Tarzan's "inhuman" plight affectively coerces her into accepting English literacy as critical to the development of the human from so-called inhuman, animal, primitive, female and other sub or nonhuman states. To construct this account of the human, Burroughs relies on modern philosophical and educational concepts of literacy that prevail in contemporary Western thought and practice. Using psychoanalytic reading, I expose the anxious lines of thinking founding dominant theories and practices of literacy that continue to underpin the colonizing imperatives of English literacy globally circulating today.

In chapter 4 I perform a close reading of J. M. Coetzee's (2003) novel and/or series of novellas, *Elizabeth Costello*. I focus, particularly, on a novella portraying the transference situation of a fictional reader that uncontrollably steers her reading. Processes of projective identification and a prior conflict with evil in the form of a violent rape resurface in the novel as Costello attempts to comprehend literary depictions of atrocity from the Holocaust. Costello's infantile conflicts with the novel surface a prior, repressed, and unthinkable experience of evil, which unknowingly interferes with her present attempt to make meaning of a novel depiction of it. I look to Freud's (1905) theory of transference to support my engagement with Costello's difficulties with symbolizing evil. Coetzee's psychical representation of Costello's inhibition with literacy offers educators a tangible encounter with the warring insides of a reader barring her efforts to communicate her experience of the other's words. From my reconstruction of Costello's grief-stricken reading experience, I call for an analytical practice of literacy attuned to microdynamics of reading and to one's inner life.

Toni Morrison's (2004) novel *Beloved* depicts how atrocity and systematic oppression can shatter one's internal world and one's relationship to language. Engaging with this novel in chapter 5, I argue that the ex-slaves' lived experiences with and in the symbolic order irreparably estrange them from language. I examine how entrenched, dehumanizing practices of literacy are implicated in nonhuman representations of black characters and in acts of mass degradation carried out by the slaveholders. Morrison indicts demeaning forms of literacy with an accompany narrative of the nonhuman in the traumatic American history of black slavery. However, Morrison also incredibly demonstrates how language, bound to psychic redevelopment imaged in poetic symbol reformation, supports Sethe in her long, slow journey to repair her inner world, to remember the past and to respond to the meanings of a deeply held within humanity. Using the novel to mirror Klein's (1937) symbolic theory of reparation and my argument that literacy can renew us from the inside out, I read and respond to the novel as performing the painful labor of psychic, social, and material restoration of recognition to the self. As characters begin to piece together their shattered realities, literary language alters an unthinkable existence in and by way of the symbolically reparative work of mourning. Engaging with and learning from the formal and aesthetic workings of Morrison's literacy of the other, teachers can begin to forge literacies that use language imaginatively and justly to respond to the past and present, unimaginable lived realities of "Others."

In the concluding chapter, I present a number of implications of this study for teachers and researchers of literacy and literature. These implications emerge from three main ways that I am rereading literacy in this study: as returning to the maternal relation; as a sustained engagement with necessary and excessive forms of language; and as repairing and renewing demeaned social life through the imaginative, internalized, and felt capacity of language. With these rereadings of the role of psychical literacy in human subject formation as depicted by literature, I lay the grounds for rewriting and practicing a literacy of the Other that poetically renarrates humanity from its troubled history of symbolically dehumanizing vulnerable lives. I suggest that literary work and imaginative language conducive to representing the inside lives of sentient creatures form the basis for renewing humanity that can bear its unspeakable history and modes of existence in the interest of creating a language that revitalizes literacy and humanizes us all.

In these six chapters, I bring psychoanalysis to postcolonial literature to generate an inner conception of literacy gifting us with recourse to symbolic meaning, as a linguistic gift bestowed upon one by the (m)other. Demeaning practices of literacy overlook the child's complex and affective relationship to language. This relationship begins at birth with one's (m)other and accompanies one's learning throughout one's life. Where and how language is implicated in the symbolic formation of sentient life is an important moment in one's ongoing struggle to apprehend forms of language that do justice to one's sense of oneself and others. Renarrating the human away from its dehumanizing metaphysical imperatives demands a *literacy of the Other.* Engaging with the indelible psychical effects of literacy constructing "fictions" of the self and societies, we are offered a chance to narrate renewed forms and contents of human existence.

1

Fictive Readings

Literacy Lessons: Nelson

Teaching abroad as a primary school teacher, I encountered an unforgettable child. The child, whom I call Nelson, was born into historical conditions of civil war and conflict in a small nation in the global South. Orphaned at birth, Nelson was adopted by Westerners. When he came to me at age seven, Nelson was precocious and emotionally expressive. Nelson took to me and I to him. As with some teaching encounters, profound was our brief time together.

Nelson was an unpredictable child. I remember waiting with some trepidation before the moments of his arrival at my class. Typically full of unfathomable rage and grief, Nelson tended to preempt my responses to his mental state with declarations such as, "I had a bad night." Evidence of the bad night emerged as Nelson lashed out his insides in our class through a fantastic barrage of words and deeds. The slightest and most benign provocation sent Nelson off into a shocking flurry of phrases and activity.

Before encountering Nelson, I was given a meeting with his previous teachers. As I took notes, I was warned that the child was "offensive," "inappropriate," and in need of "professional help." I was told not to tolerate his bad behavior. In that meeting both Nelson and I were put on notice: he was to behave and I was to ensure his good behavior. At stake was my credibility as a teacher and Nelson's membership into the community of the international school. After the meeting, I realized that not a single word was uttered about the child's well-being or how I might support his learning.

Viewing his small, painfully wire-thin body for the first time, I wondered what on earth this tiny Nelson did to provoke such hostile responses from the adults entrusted with his care. In teacher's college my classmates and I had learned to label this kind of child behaviorally disturbed. Accompanying Nelson on his frequent trips to the school psychologist, I learned that the official diagnosis for such a child is "oppositional defiance disorder," although this was just the main one of many labels the psychologist rapidly interspersed for various behaviors Nelson exhibited. Surprisingly, the school team rarely spoke of Nelson's formative histories or of his adoption by Westerners. The version of Nelson's story I received came mostly from him. Through his rapid self-disclosures I learned that from birth Nelson had suffered numerous losses of primary attachments to people and places. In my mind, this social devastation, so painfully articulated by Nelson, was a root cause of his distress. Also overlooked was the fact of Nelson's "foreign" racial and ethnic status within his adopted family and nation and new school and country. Rather than confront Nelson's personal situation, our team meetings on "the problem of Nelson" bracketed out any conversation we might have had on how to support his emotional development in the wake of a volatile past. Instead, the meetings centered mainly on teaching *me* a series of decontextualized labels and strategies, as this was the school's only method of containing Nelson's uncontrollable outbursts in the classroom.

Even before I attempted to support Nelson, I had a feeling that the strategies the psychologist offered would be of little help. Nelson did not fit the character that educational labels sought to qualify. I saw him as an extremely bright, deeply troubled boy whose forms of learning required a creative response. To the psychologist's dismay, the parents refused pharmaceutical intervention. And no matter how hard he tried in countless sessions with Nelson, the child's emotional disturbances seemed to elude the expert knowledge of this well-intended but heavy-handed psychologist. I remember Nelson declaring eloquently, to the psychologist's chagrin: "I do not actually require gold stars. I am not a circus animal."

The year progressed and Nelson showed no visible signs of improvement. The team of experts working with him for more than three years found themselves at a complete loss. They considered ejecting Nelson from the school. They might have if not for his parents' elevated social standing within the community, my determination to support the child, and my principal's sympathy for the child's plight. In a last ditch effort to save their child, the parents, frustrated with the school system, quite naturally turned on me. They cited Nelson's trouble as my failure as his teacher. Their summation held up; after all, I had little prior knowledge and experience for managing a child deemed as difficult as Nelson.

In a bid to protect myself as I protected the child, I began to cover up Nelson's outbursts. I closed my door to professional help. I assured the team that Nelson was making progress even though he clearly was not. My principal seemed to silently share my capacity for good humor and imagination as resources for teaching Nelson. Without explicit approval, he supported my maternal inclination toward the child and left me alone to work with Nelson. Left to my own devices, I rejected the help and suggestions of colleagues and searched within for a pedagogy by which I could reach Nelson.

Self-exiled from the school community and my colleagues, I retreated inside myself and away from my teacher training. There, I rediscovered a slew of memories of another, less violently displaced child. This verbally precocious child of melancholic immigrant South Asians learned to navigate inhospitable territory with her father's thick *Webster's Dictionary* in hand. Into my deeply affected response to Nelson's emotional turmoil, I transferred my father's imperative to exploit English, hoping to turn it to Nelson's advantage. I began fashioning spectacular narratives to soothe his conflict waged with words. Through these words, of displacement, journey, estrangement, and belonging, he began to puzzle together a story that plausibly represented his inconsolable losses of formative people and places.

Even with sustained support, Nelson continued to exhibit difficulty when expressing his need. Communication of his deepest frustrations curiously paralleled his strategic use of offensive verbal expressions. His rabid verbiage consisted of a surprising yet necessary defense of himself. Nelson's jarring speech, deemed inappropriate by his guardians and teachers, had the effect of barring those who might help him. His cries for help were drowned out by his brazen and rude use of language. Through the language warfare he enacted, Nelson successfully managed to repel anyone coming remotely close to his stealthily protected insides. He repetitively informed people, "I'm not who you think I am," using existential deferral as a shield to navigate his way in a hostile world.

My creative intervention with the child hinged on his off-putting expressions of existence. I latched onto his forms of speech, and, together, we began to imaginatively unravel each detail of his shocking symbolic constructions. I viewed these strange expressions as Nelson's psychical[1] literacy: his unique idiom, accent, and incredible inner means of formally structuring fragments of thought in strange poetic form. With the hindsight of constructs offered to me by psychoanalysis, I now interpret Nelson's powerful and precocious use of English as the sole means by which he resiliently and quite brilliantly expressed a semblance of his incomprehensible beginnings. His symbolic constructions uncannily mirrored his existential crises and became his problem of learning. Nelson had trouble observing time, forming attachments to curricular objects, containing emotions, and ordering his thoughts in appropriate forms of discourse. He showed other signs of learning distress through his strange somatic behaviors. He gnawed on his fingers and pencil. He shouted at ghosts inside and outside of the classroom. He pleaded with fantasized demons to "get off him." Rather than punish, I took his words and returned to him new and gentler versions of his trouble. I realized that every wish to drive away others held a wish for them to never let him go. My careful response offered back to his repulsive language words that soothed a constant fear of being left behind. Nelson's constructions, so frightening to him and others, found in my vocabulary of belonging, softer forms of life that he began to trust. I was consistently hospitable to his relentless expressions of seething rage because the, at times, intolerable barrage of words and uncontrollable behaviors gave me insight into his shaking mental state.

From our symbolic interactions I learned that Nelson experienced, on a daily basis, inner conflicts that ruined his attempts to form a communicable and reliable self, which he needed to relate and be recognizable to others. I taught the children in my classroom that there was nothing to fear from Nelson's words as "they are 'just words' after all" (Farley 2012, 175). Words could hurt, I explained to their openly concerned faces, and at the same time, words were Nelson's only way to hold down and chase away his hurt. The children came to see that they were not the intended targets of the need to injure that lay behind Nelson's words. Following my very calm and contained lead, the children began to normalize Nelson's presence and his odd way of speaking his truth. As the year progressed, I became increasingly convinced that Nelson's strange use of language, which caused all of us so much grief, was the only thing keeping his fragile mind and existence afloat. He needed an unfathomably defensive vocabulary to navigate the stormy social seas threatening to subsume a complicated existence.

A beginning teacher with little experience and no special education training, I drew my ideas on creatively supporting Nelson's language trouble directly from a literary education. I decided to use Nelson's highly literate capacity for symbolically waging the war within as a way to generate and renew the child's obvious intellectual brilliance and imaginative capacity. I followed the free-floating form of his affect and read Nelson's attempts to communicate as novel constructions. I received his words as a fabulous fiction of a wounded self not meant to harm others. I did not view Nelson's linguistic outbursts as a personal threat against his classmates and myself or against the educational enterprise, as did the indignant psychologist. I began to observe how his somewhat ironic, overdramatic, subversive, and vastly humorous usages of language offered me a sliver of insight into his highly charged mental state.

Out of my need for sheer survival as a beginning teacher, I created a literary method of reading the child's emotional state as he expressed it through what the psychologist documented as, "Nelson's bizarre use of language." Combining my training as both a scholar of English literature and a teacher of young children, I did not take Nelson at his word but at what I could feel driving his words: an unfathomable emotional content compelling him to verbally fend off anyone who tried to come close. I began to imaginatively feel my way into Nelson's unique way of expelling his ideas and the world as a guide to reading his unreadable insides. Some of the social justice education methods I had acquired as a pre-service student helped me spur Nelson's interest in various kinds of curriculum. But, it was my affective and literary analysis of the form and content in which his expressions arrived that offered me the most possibilities for teaching Nelson.

To this day, I am unsure of the long-term effect of my interventions on Nelson's development. As with many teachers' memories of students, the real child Nelson exists now as a fiction I create through the auspices of unreliable memory. Yet, in our pedagogical encounter I witnessed significant change in Nelson's responses to himself, to others in the classroom, and to his teachers. The psychologist and his parents discredited the interventions I stubbornly developed and used to support Nelson's literacy development, citing my lack of emotional distance, experience, and expertise. But they could not deny that my teaching, experimental as charged, affected a change in Nelson. I observed Nelson using my words to briefly find moments of emotional balance. I witnessed him using interpretive and imaginative forms of language. I noticed how creative forms of language supported him to loosen his tight attachment to impoverished and demeaning vocabulary of images of himself offered to him by adults. I realized that the negative representations of Nelson authored by adults and teachers left him with no viable way to represent his inner life and impermissible lived experiences. Labels, categories, and disciplinary actions continued to hold him to account for a person that was not, in the first place, fashioned on his terms of existence. Finding relief in a story of existence that no longer resembled the one causing him no end to grief, Nelson clung to our co-constructed, emotionally rich, and open narrative of self. He grew less impulsive and defensive as he became more adept with interpreting and representing his ideas and thoughts to others. With his expanding vocabulary, he achieved moments of emotional and behavioral balance with others. From the new story of Nelson that we recreated together from what we imagined his insides were trying to say, Nelson gained some balanced insight into how to use words to express and manage the ravages of his inside life and precious mind.

My encounter with a child almost twenty years ago, when I was young and without children of my own, reminds me to take seriously a person's psychical life as fundamental for supporting his literacy. This child literally needed sympathetic words in the form of a caring and analytic vocabulary to attend to a daily experienced and inconsolable grief. Using the alter-existential vocabulary I offered, Nelson learned to read and write his painful inside life into a recognizable linguistic form that acknowledged his internal injuries. He needed a responsive and hospitable language: his existence and lifelong relation to others depended upon it. With my sustained literary attention to his broken symbolic formations, I was able to support Nelson's beginning capacity to read and write of a self that accorded to the internal map of language learning with which I imagined his mother had gifted him in infancy. The socializing forms of literacy offered to Nelson by his parents, school, and society were hostile to his primal need to acknowledge and respond to his terrible feelings of loss of primary people and places. Loss raging within expressed itself through his desperate need to articulate his truth. Using the symbolically reparative process of signifying and resignifying a ruined inside world, Nelson embarked on a relentless internal quest for justice in the wake of real and imagined injuries he suffered at the hands of somewhat merciless social beginnings. As a child of enormous privilege, Nelson wanted for nothing materially, and yet his insides remained impoverished by the discourses available to articulate his ruined existence. To have a chance to live a life with meaningful potential required interpretive openness and a literacy that responded to and represented his lived realities.

Lessons learned from Nelson sustained my literacy teaching with children and adults in the long term. I learned, much later during my doctorate and with some narcissistic shame, that my wild pedagogical experiments with the inner literate life of children was not my invention: child psychoanalysts in centuries past had developed multiple tried and tested methods for reading and analyzing the child's psychical literacy through her symptoms, silences, volatile behaviors, and cryptic words and deeds. Freud's observations on the founding children of psychoanalysis, his grandson Ernst and "Little Hans," opened the door to a new psychoanalytic field, child analysis. In this field, clues in the child's emotional expressions and behavioral responses came to present children's lives lived from the inside out. The child analyst's experimental orientation to reading the child's inner world appealed to my literary efforts to pedagogically intervene in the child's disturbing verbal and written expression.

When I first read of Melanie Klein's analytical efforts with a child named "Richard," I was overwhelmed with memories of Nelson. As with Nelson, Richard was wracked with deep fear and anxiety at the thought of threats to his existence. Troubled by the sights and sounds of World War II during the Blitz over the English countryside, Richard became uncommunicative. Their child's deep and unreachable distress compelled Richard's parents to seek help from Klein. Describing him as a "bright and precocious" child, Klein intuitively knew that Richard's inhibition with others could not be attributed to a mental or behavioral deficiency (Klein 1961, 15). Her carefully narrated analytic technique with Richard demonstrates Klein's commitment to supporting the child's well-being through language development. Her inventive interpretations of Richard's trouble, still subject to heated debate in the adult community of analysts, spoke to the child from the inside out.

To my great surprise, Klein preferred working with children exhibiting delays and disturbances with symbolic communication. She viewed behavioral difficulties in children as a problem of communication and traced its emotional path back to the child's infantile experiences with mother. She refused to deem emotionally disturbed children as behaviorally deviant, pathological, or abnormal, as is too commonly the case in education. Instead, she used the word *inhibited* to describe children who routinely struggled to manage emotions and behavior. She attributed the child's struggles to an impaired capacity to express his need and/or self.

Resonating with Klein's deeply sympathetic and open orientation to the internal worlds of children, I was driven to read all of her cases. I discovered that my literary efforts to read the inside lives of children had a home in child psychoanalysis. In Klein's cases, I was given relief from pedagogical solitary confinement in a profession unable to bear a teacher's intuitive and emotional experimentation with the inner conflicts of children. My literary pedagogy with Nelson resounded in Klein's cases firmly equipped with a documented vocabulary mapping out the rocky royal road of the child's fictive inner life.

My faltering pedagogy, not quite psychoanalytic—I did not have the authority, language, or training—was aligned with the methods of child psychoanalysis. As in psychoanalysis, literacy of the Other attunes its ear to the child's insides. To pedagogically support a literacy of the Other, the teacher gains insight into the individual child's informal methods for language learning by engaging her emotional expressions. These aesthetic expressions hold insight into the complex workings of the child's internal life. From my work with children I find that early childhood literacy requires the teacher to engage the child's compulsion to symbolize as first and foremost an internal situation. I call the child's felt, internal situation waiting to be symbolically expressed *psychical literacy*. As I learned from Nelson, a pedagogy oriented to the child's inner world can support teachers to foster an interpretive response to her language triumphs and problems.

Klein's Object Relations: Psychical Literacy

Along with finding its inspiration in Nelson and other elementary school children who exhibit inhibitions with literacy, the psychical theory of literacy I advance in this book emerges from the work of Melanie Klein. An "indisputable figure" in psychoanalysis, Klein dedicated her life's work to supporting the child's inner sense of self through various interpretive forms of symbolic play and communication (Kristeva 2001, 6). Born in Vienna to assimilated Jews in 1882, and married with three children, Klein suffered bouts of debilitating depression throughout her life. In 1910 she began an analysis with Sandor Ferenczi, a key figure in the psychoanalytic archive and close contemporary of Freud. Through these sessions, Ferenczi came to the conclusion that Klein had a "gift with children" (Kristeva 2001, 26). Ferenczi encouraged Klein to analyze her own children as the training ground for her theory and practice of child analysis. From Klein's observations on and analysis of inhibited children emerged a technique for child analysis still used by clinicians and educators today.

Klein remains an unorthodox and controversial figure in psychoanalytic circles. Recently, in the fields of education and social theory, there is renewed interest in her ideas. Still, her conception of the infant-maternal relation has yet to find educational impact. Little scholarly attention continues to be afforded to the profound yet completely forgettable scene of maternal literacy (Grumet 1988). Throughout this book I return to Klein's study of the internal mechanisms of infants as fundamental to one's capacity to symbolically communicate one's existence to others. These infantile mechanisms prepare the grounds for verbal literacy and its variants and support our subsequent sophisticated practices of symbolic communication. Radically, Klein's theory of object relations reconstructs literacy development as vital to one's chance to construct and narrate both one's own humanity and that of others. Literacy's role in subject formation expands the current view of literacy as merely an educational or cultural achievement necessary for human progress, societal participation, and/or material and economic well-being.

For Klein, natality marks one's fall into a psychical condition imbued with meaning. Psychoanalyst Gregory Kohon describes the infant's prelinguistic condition as already symbolically significant:

> Even before the infant can understand language, before he has developed his capacity for linguistic expression (one could argue, even before his birth), he lives in a cultural milieu, which provides a context and extensive references to his existence. We are conceived, born, and exist in a world of others; it is these relationships that give meaning to our lives. These subjects are desiring subjects, who impose their own linguistic code on the newly arrived. The baby arrives to a meaningful world, marked and defined by language. . . . The baby falls into a world of significant others; mother, father, grandparents, with their own desires and their histories, their dreams and their own personal myths.

> The baby is to discover that, prior to his birth, he has been existing in the minds of others; he has been given a name, has become part of a myth determined by others' desires. The world that welcomes him belongs to others; there will always be a considerable *plus* of signification that the baby will not be able to decode. (Kohon 2005, 46)

As Kohon indicates, the infant is meaning-full at birth. She is an absorbent, fleshy, sensate creature submerged in the sounds and sights of a foreign world filled to the brim with words that mean. The baby's first, fleeting, aural and tactile sense of the world outside the self resounds in the child's internal capacity to make sense, meaning, and interpretation of her lived condition. The *plus*, or excess of signification, to which Kohon refers is the unconscious and affective material structuring meaning that the baby takes in as she encounters objects from the external world. The (m)other's desire for the baby is imprinted in language and begins to "make" of the baby what it will in the name of culture, religion, and the nation. The excesses of signification traced in the first narrative of baby given to her by others are deposited into the baby's unconscious. These unconscious affects support one's lifelong mental functioning and well-being.

Klein's oeuvre acknowledges the profound role of maternity in the mental and symbolic development of the child. Taking in sounds and gestures, the infant is unequipped to speak at birth. Without the benefit of intelligible spoken language, the infant's capacity for communication consists of her flaying efforts to wordlessly express to mother a total sense of an internally felt existence. Communication might seem next to impossible for the nonverbal tiny human. And yet, as Klein convincingly argues, the infant's prelingual state does not dissuade her compulsion to communicate with mother. In infancy, communication with mother consists of a mysterious communion of inside lives conveyed mostly through feeling. Relying completely on internally felt impressions, the infant expresses her overwhelming need to mother who must then interpret these expressions and respond well to her unspeakable situation. The child's first somatic efforts to communicate to mother are animated in this unconscious, mute, immemorial time of infant-mother communion.

The infant's compulsion to symbolize begins at birth with her fragile efforts to communicate to others a sense of dire need.[2] Without words, and clinging to the mother's care, the infant is nonetheless incredibly capable of intracommunication that belies empirical determinations of human thought and language. Upon birth the infant gives a sense of her instinct to survive through her first gasps, cries, and grunts. Felt expressions of need activate the child's innate capacities for sense making. In turn, the pressing need to communicate drives the infant's first "phantastic" capacity to "mentalize" and express her felt reality to mother.

Klein claims the baby's need to express her mental state coincides with the first feeding experience: "I found that object relations start almost at birth and arise with the first feeding experience; furthermore, that all aspects of mental life are bound up with object relations" (Klein 1955, 52). She (1928) identified the breast as the first object to which the baby is indelibly attached. Kristeva suggests that the infant's sensational drive to the breast conjures a phantastic mental state, which forms the basis of her mental life.

> The *sensation of a drive* in the psychic apparatus is automatically associated with the fantasy of an *object* that is appropriated to it, with each incitement of the drives having its own corresponding fantasy (the desire for food, for example, is associated with the affect of hunger and the breast object). From the moment of birth, the drive engages in a binary expression: sensation/affect and the object both *co-exist,* and the presentation of the object clings to sensation. The Kleinian phantasy is the mechanism of this juncture, of the drives' destiny to be both inside and outside: it is an "object-seeking" drive. (Kristeva 2001, 141–42)

Through phantasy,[3] the baby associates the drive to a corresponding mental status of the object whose character is felt, imagined, and expressed. The internal sensation conflated with the actual mother's breast is psychically managed, deposited, and traced in the unconscious. Mentally taking in (introjection) and putting out (projection) objects/breast initiates the infant's first visually mental efforts for making sense. She expresses these sensations through unintelligible symbolic forms such as crying, screaming, gurgling, or sighing, The mentally experienced feeding event parallels the actual phenomenon of taking in sustenance. The two processes, psychical and social, only partially correspond and easily set each other off track and into opposition. In phantasy, it is as if the baby, completely from within, is put upon to manage and operate within two parallel universes competing for the infant's attention and desire.

Internally making relations to the mother's breast gives the child her first felt, hostile, and gratifying experience of the external world. Her need of others animates feelings of terror, persecution, grief, and gratitude toward those entrusted with her care. In turn, these feelings build up and lay down the infant's psyche:

> The object-world of the child in the first two or three months of its life could be described as consisting of hostile and persecuting, or else of gratifying parts and portions of the real world. Before long the child perceives more and more of the whole person of the mother, and this more realistic perception extends to the whole world beyond the mother. The fact that a good relation to its mother and to the external world helps the baby to overcome its early paranoid anxieties throws a new light on the importance of its earliest experiences. (Klein 1935, 141)

This fraught stage of mental development consists of the infant's internal breakdown of total objects into good and bad to gain control over the sensations the objects present. Through this process of disintegration of objects the baby is given the capacity to mentalize more manageable bits and pieces of perceptions of external reality. These bits and pieces are integrated as a form of infantile sense making. The communal process by which the baby learns to internalize and project external objects forms the basis for her symbolic capacity to make sense of people and things. As she begins to discern between feeling and object, the baby stabilizes her fraught relation to mother. Before long, the baby integrates her feelings for the mother as a whole person rather than in bits and pieces of love and hate.

The precariousness of infancy and mental development relies on how well the infant manages and makes sense of the all-encompassing bits of part objects and people with and without the other's support. Accordingly, the mother plays a fundamental role in laying down the meaning-making system in the infant. The mother's response to the infant's fragile and repeated attempts to communicate her split sense of her self supports the baby's unique way of managing, ordering, and integrating internally felt sensations and objects.

Even when the baby begins to discern the mother as a whole person, split feeling conveying the baby's need for her qualifies the infant's first sense of the world. Babies cry all the time to convey grief at their existential condition of total dependence on others and objects. When we interpret the baby's communication as sad, we mistake the infant's prelinguistic grief for an emotion that is not yet a distinct symbol with a moral orientation. Infantile grief is not sad, mad, or bad. Grief instead supports an emerging, complex, and phantastic mental state. Prelingual grief contains a vast set of splitting meanings that reach beyond a simple emotional signification such as sad.

For the baby, the object becomes subject to her feeling for it, and feeling is both fickle and fleeting. Within seconds, the object world can fantastically go from feeling good to feeling bad for the baby. These sharp fluctuations of the infant's split mental state greatly impact on the mother's effort to locate the source of the infant's distress. The mother's "body reading" of infantile expression can become confused and confuse and is prone to misreading (Grumet 1988). Unable to gauge or attend to what she thinks the infant needs, the mother can regress into her own infancy. With the infantile regression, the mother also experiences splitting and unspeakable forms of grief. She can also mistake pleasure for pain and pain for pleasure. During this overwhelming, confused, perpetually in crisis activity of splitting correspondence between self, sensations, and object/other, the inner world is built up as the infant's mechanism for integrating sense is laid down. As the mother begins to carefully and consistently respond to the baby's need, the baby's split sense of herself becomes more balanced and more readily able to take in new people and things.

These first sets of wild and devastating misreadings taking place between infant and mother in the infantile scene is unconsciously transferred to the child's subsequent readings of objects, others, and the world. The anxious and explicitly grief-stricken efforts to make psychical relation to each other lay down and build up an interperceptive apparatus upon which the child will build her evolving co-authored interpretive capacities. This infantile register supports one, across a lifetime, to read the world according to unconscious and prior experiences of her self.

Profound, felt, and phantastic communication between mother and infant comprise the internal activities of psychical literacy. Kristeva (2001) deems this communication semiotic, likening it to Plato's *chora,* a collaborative and fictive communication with (m)other emitted in rhythms, tones, inflection, and murmuring. The communication is also sensual; we speak with eyes against eyes, breath against eyelash, skin against skin, mouth against nipple. We gain a sense of the unbearable qualities of this kind of communication when, as adults, we feel split apart, when aggression and feelings of hate emerge, when meaning breaks down and we are unable to find words to express our trouble.

In his writing on the not known of thinking, Derrida (1976a) characterizes this form of infantile communication as arche-writing, Arche writing refers to the bare trace of unconscious drives and desires left behind in the linguistic structure we use to piece together existential thoughts of ourselves and others. As philosophical thought is consumed with thoughts of existence, it is most prone to infantile feelings. Arche-writing, Derrida insists, precedes existential writing because, "It is that very thing that cannot let itself be reduced to the form of presence" (1976a, 57). The term *arche* suggests an originary source for writing that is necessary or involved in the practice of making symbolic meaning. Arche-writing resembles psychical literacy, although Derrida himself only refers to this writing in terms of the trace it leaves behind, "not only in the form and substance of graphic expression but also in those of nongraphic expression" (ibid., 60). In his conception of trace, Derrida's conception of arche-writing in philosophy uncannily resembles Klein's theory of psychical literacy. Both Derrida and Klein suggest that psychical traces of formative others drive one's symbolic expressions and interpretations of others.[4] And as Derrida finds in his deconstruction of the great metaphysical texts, traces of a thinker's thoughts can resemble the stuff of Kleinian phantasy.

In stark contrast to the dependent structure of existence driving psychical literacy, the symbolic order is primarily used to privilege the self over others. Speaking gives way to naming. Naming alienates mother and child. The violent opposing of self and other is instituted upon the child's aural and oral determination that she is "I" and mother is "other than I."[5] But this sovereignty that language institutes is illusory. In Western thought, Lévinas (1969) writes, "I" as sovereign Self is overdetermined to the point that man mythically believes himself to be omnipotent and with no need for others. This idea is fundamentally misleading because, as Klein insists, human subjectivity is continuously forming in response to our need of (m)others. The maternal relation evidences this dependent structure of human existence. Although the first scene of reading is foreclosed in the child's learning to speak and then read and write print, it never leaves. Each time we struggle to make meaning we are reminded of infantile need. Our need of the other is embedded in the formation of the self even while language (of self) gives us the illusion of separateness, of sovereignty.

Klein's theory of object relations is critical to my reconstruction of literacy because it situates meaning making in the (m)other rather than the word. The (m)other is there before I am. She receives me into a world of words. Meaning making in this earliest human relation stresses the bodily felt and articulated co-constructed experience of language learning. Object relations ground the formation of human thought in preconscious mental activity. This mental activity is experienced first in the body in the mouth, skin/nipple, and ear. Rather than attribute our first meaning-making experiences to our entry into the patriarchal symbolic order, Klein's theory suggests that our need of others gives way to our expressive capacity to wordlessly communicate ourselves to others. This capacity, this mysterious internal intelligence, gives way to "wording," to language learning (Bollas 1999).

Klein is reluctant to equate literacy with the empire and empiricism of speaking. Instead, she looks to affect, gesture, emotion, expression, idiom, outburst as guides to words that contain the child's infantile impressions of formative people and things. These internalized impressions are traced in the words that the child uses to express an existential sense of herself to others. The child's need of words is as sweet nourishment and bitter milk (Grumet 1988). Words imbued with felt meanings feed her capacity to elaborate upon an incredible existential sense of self and other in spectacular, fantastic, and symbolic forms of knowledge, art, culture, and civilization. As we become schooled in literacy, poet Shel Silverstein laments, we forget the inner language of communion with others needed to speak to unspeakable things inside ourselves. His poem "Forgotten Language" poignantly recalls the child's capacity to "speak the language of the flowers" and "understand each word the caterpillar said" (Silverstein 1974, 149). The infant-child's inner capacity to commune with the insides of speaking and nonspeaking others forms the basis of the psychical life of literacy; a trace of its unconscious activity stirs in the child's unique idiom and expression that accompany her through a lifelong relationship through language. We can never quite let go of our capacities to phantasize and feel the insides of the world out.

I stumbled on the incredible resource of the child's inner life when attempting to support the literacy development of Nelson. In my teaching of young children, I was often moved to think again when confronted with their fantastic uses of symbolic constructions. I strained to hear the yearning and mournful communication behind a child's affect-driven words. Using literary training, I read the force of feeling behind the child's tremendous efforts to communicate. Fictive readings of the child's inner life can move us to imagine an earlier time when words were hard and we had few resources for speaking of our felt human condition. Communing with the child's spectacular fantastic insides supports her to develop and contain emotionally wrought processes of symbolization.

At and after birth the infant is subject to a number of intense experiences that are laden with the mother's power, symbolism, and significance taken in and projected out by the baby. Infancy provides the child with a chance to become both herself and other than herself. How she negotiates competing demands to exist depends on the adult reception of her body in a world premade with meanings and significations. The literate means and modes by which the mother pedagogically brings the infant precariously into a world of words is critical to her subject formation. Throughout this book, I demonstrate how Nelson's psychically fragmented questions of self, other and world, history, justice and repair fueling his symbolic constructions vividly appear in the psychic life of children's literacy, the writings of Klein and Derrida, and literature that grapples with the mysteries of existence. In the next chapter, I will suggest that the infant's forgotten language has a markedly literary quality. I look to literature to develop further the idea of fictive reading as gaining the capacity to feel for or follow the fragile lines of the other's mental efforts to communicate a sense of herself to others. Readers, teachers, and scholars can develop this capacity to feel one's way through text with support of psychoanalytic constructs mapping out the emotional life. Engaging our felt readings of literature can tentatively open up an imaginative mode of affectively reading the world and others. Reading with feeling might support us to carefully re-narrate the fictional forms of knowledge by which we stake claims to the world and others. We might then begin to recognize the immense existential significance of the (m)other's literacy that forms the facts of our social condition as it provides fictive conditions for social life.

2

Literary Stirrings

The Inner Life of Literacy

My compulsion to engage the other's passionate efforts to communicate is animated by a childhood immersed in the voices of second-language learners. Early on in life, I learned to read the other's inner world through an immersion in my mother's emotionally delivered, half-broken English. In my mother's labored efforts to speak in a language that betrayed her insides, I witnessed how closely tied is the other's inner life to her effort to communicate. Unraveling the tangled knot between a person's feelings and words is key to my psychosocial reconstruction of literacy.

As I embarked on formal literary training, my interpretations of canonical texts stubbornly relied on my childhood efforts to unravel the psychical details lodged in my mother's strange, jarring, and poetic symbolic formations. This penetrating style of reading continues to inform my trained interpretations of social and literary texts. I use a sophisticated yet quasi-analytical form of inside reading as a guide when navigating novel constructions formed by tiny people, educational theorists, and literary and social texts.

My felt analysis of the novel did not serve me well in the English literature classroom. I was considered a bad student during my English undergrad because my unconventional readings of the novel tended to conflict with the professor's interpretation. Despite eagerly learning to acquire a strong sense of the formal and aesthetic movement of novels, my readings invariably got stuck in the unspoken emotional content of the narrative. Professors constantly took me to task for misreading literary tropes, vocabulary, devices, and methods used by the writer. "You need to learn how to read," one brusquely informed me. No matter how hard I tried close reading in accordance with the esteemed English professor's instructions, I faltered, with interpretation wavering along the psychical interference I felt circulating between the writer, the text, and myself.

My interpretations became the target of the English professor's incredulity. I was deemed wild, untrained, and belligerent for my persistence in forging what RM Kennedy (2011) terms an "unclassical retrieval" of the humanist novel. Yet, quite remarkably, my speculative form of inside reading was generative in the early childhood literacy classroom. There, I put a failed English education to use and began conducting felt "readings" of the child's frustrated and fantastic attempt to communicate. I took childish feelings as a guide for their literacy. I attended to the child's thoughts and feelings when immersed in literacy activities. I consulted some children in one on one interviews on their feelings while learning how to read and write. And I scoured children's symbolic representations—visual, verbal, and in print—for clues on their evolving relations to literacy.

After leaving the elementary school classroom, I discovered that my pedagogical use of the emotional worlds of children's literacy roughly resembled the analytic technique of child psychoanalyst Melanie Klein. When engaging children's communications, Klein took as a guide their emotional expressions. She analyzed their verbal, visual, and written attempts to symbolize their thoughts. From her analysis of children's nonsensical talk and behaviors, Klein created a vibrant emotional vocabulary and set of analytical constructs with which to make visible the inner lives of infants and young children.

The inner life of the child is a borderline space between the unconscious, fantasized, and representable thoughts of the child. It can be hard to gain a sense of the inner life, as it feels nonsensical. The inner life can also grant us a much-needed retreat from the pressing demands of reality. It offers us an escape from reality. The inner life transports us to a space of wishes, reverie, and daydreams that we can entertain in silence and secret. Perhaps we are closest to our inner lives when we are daydreaming unencumbered by our education and social ties and free to engage illicit desires, secret worlds, and unconscious wishes.

Along with its presence in the emotional expressions of infants and children, we can find traces of the inner life of literacy in the aesthetic form, content, and reception of some literary works. As with the maternal relation, literature holds the inner lives of both the writer and the reader in an unspoken demand to communicate. Daniel Coleman suggests that reading generates a spiritual communion between reader and writer. Reading immerses the self in the fictional world of the other. Reading, Coleman writes, "consists of a strange paradox in which readers imagine themselves to be entering the mental world of the author precisely in the author's absence" (Coleman 2009, 78). Writing a text to be read by another, the author, too, must imagine himself entering the mental world of the reader entirely in her absence. In this communion of pressing inner lives without bodies, the novel provides a fleeting meeting space. The space is one of communication where one is not bodily bound to the other and yet is temporally bound to her words. The novel's effect on a person falls between fantasy and reality, between psychical and literary production and reception, between reader and writer.

In my work, *pedagogic* is the word I use to describe the inner communion of inner meaningful exchange between two people. When reading, we can temporarily ruin and renew a sense of ourselves in thoughts of each other. Author and reader are affected by an intense correspondence in mind where two strangers, without speaking to each other, intimately communicate, teach, and learn and make meaning. The exchange of meaning generated by the novel can produce a profound form of literary pedagogy.

Judith Robertson suggests that literary pedagogy counts on the imaginative potential of words to produce an embodied event of meaningful exchange. Engagement with exemplary literary works can support teachers of literacy and literature to attend to the learner's inner life in language development and the creative possibilities for meaning such development promises. Although many scholars acknowledge the role of literature in literacy, they do not examine literature for its potential in literacy pedagogy. They do not think: engagements in literature can support my teaching. These lessons are not didactic. Literature's significance for education is not via application. Novels need to be mined for the insights into children's literacy they hold. Robertson writes that, taking pedagogical lessons from a novel, teachers might

> [i]magine the classroom as a canvas or holding place upon which disturbed readers can project fragmented colors of

> the mind. . . . Reading literature must be comprehended as a potentially disturbing psychic event. The openness of texts, and the interminable ambiguity of making meaning around them needs to be accepted as part of the terrain of teaching literature. (Robertson 1999, 290)

The child's efforts to communicate the meaning of their literary engagements make examinable for teachers the student's projected colors of the mind. But to gain a sense of the qualities of language learning and literature "as a psychic event," teachers might also need to read existentially challenging novels. These readings are less about ascertaining the right or correct interpretation of the novel. Instead, we read difficult works to regain a sense of the child's first faltering efforts for meaning. Novels that make us think support us to re-find the contours of our forgotten internal world. The form and content of such novels press the teacher to read like a child for existential significance. Developing the capacity to follow the formal and aesthetic operations of a novel containing the meaning of another's world supports us to gain an inner sense of the intricacies of signification. In a novel, we can be surprised to find our tightly contained desires and wishes released by the other's words.

What is existentially hard need not be overly intellectualized. The ordinary plight of Max, the main character in Maurice Sendak's children's book *Where the Wild Things Are*, poignantly illustrates this point. Banished by his mother to his room without dinner, Max embarks on an inner voyage to distant lands where he slays the monsters of his mind. These monsters emerge in an aggression erupting in Max when his mother, annoyed with his behavior, sends him away. Isolated from the world and left to his own internal devices, Max conjures a fantastic land. In his fantasy, he is master of a new society void of parents and people. Here in uncharted territory, Max is free to roam the dangerous contours of his internal world where anger can be flung out at others. But as Max stomps through this wild and solitary place, he is plagued by the loneliness of living with demons. His omnipotence grows short-lived when he realizes his tyrannical reign as king of the wild things is unfulfilling. Too long inside himself, he becomes hungry, tired, and lonely for home. Stumbling on the truth of his need and longing for his (m)other, Max returns to the world from his fantasy "rumpus" renewed with new wording possibilities the wild things offer for an altered relation to others.

Sendak's strikingly simple picture book, beloved by children across the globe, takes seriously the child's inner life as critical to her well-being and worded sense of self. The journey upon which Max embarks is totally inside. Sendak's language depicting the internal world is sparse and uncomplicated. Yet the care he takes in the selection and placement of words uncannily animates a fantastic place of childhood that feels all too real. Max's small and childish feelings of rejection, omnipotence, anger, and defeat are given a much-needed voice in Sendak's pages. And yet these feelings are not idealized nor disparaged. Instead Sendak's grief-stricken rendition of Max's ruined and remade self unexpectedly surprises because Max's need of his mother can remind us of our own: "And Max, the king of all wild things, was lonely and wanted to be where someone loved him best of all" (Sendak 2000, 29). These words, gingerly signaling the raucous journey's end, qualify the insight both the child character and the reader gain from Max's triumphant inner world adventure. The words and images Sendak uses to characterize the demons and treasures of Max's inner world are designed to appeal to the child reader's fraught sense of occupying an inside self at war with her anxious attachments and need to belong to others. When children read these words they feel or relive an experience they know all too well. More than this: through their reading children are given language with which to imagine their own treacherous journeys to the traitorous feelings simmering in their inside worlds. Literary language makes it possible for Max to soothe his demons with words and images that express the more inexpressible fears and fantasies of his existence.

Most children readily identify with Max's fantastic internal voyage. Sendak's use of language depicts, with startling familiarity, the terrors of punishment and abandonment experienced by human beings at various moments in their lives. A vocabulary of inner life bursting with incredible illustrations supports children in making sense of complex intra and interpersonal realities. It is not so much that Sendak depicts the child's inner reality; he imagines instead what words might give to a possible interpretation of an inside world of an ordinary child named Max. The child within the writer's animated internal world is transferred to the character Max. Literature stages a transference where the character taps into the writer's inside, which in turn taps into the reader's inside. This extraordinary transference between real and fictional life does not produced an actual child or childhood: Max is not literally the inner child of Maurice in this story. Instead, transferred to the adult-formed character Max is an internal and enduring remnant of Sendak's remembered idea of childhood. Sendak's memory, producing the transference figure Max, incredibly animates the reader's childhood. Literature then can be conceived as an intertextual, transference experience that moves writer, reader, and fictional character to a prior time and story inside her self.

Our lives take on new meaning as we learn to symbolize ourselves from the inside out. In contrast, literacy as an instrumental and compartmentalized set of skills voids the textured, existential significance derived from language usage, which further denies children the most vital and perhaps generative part of their communicative capacity: their fantastic, emotional life. Rather than speak of literacy, Klein termed the process by which one feels, finds and uses words to communicate inside matters to others *symbolization*. Symbolization, as a psychosocial process of meaning making navigating the thin line of psychical and social life, characterizes the immense internal effort required to turn felt things into words. Symbolic literacy as produced from the child's phantastic internal world is a radical idea that can orient educators toward the significance of the inner life in the child's production of meaning.

Symbolization: Psychical Literacy

Symbolization follows the unconscious processes of meaning competing with and producing communicable forms of discourse. For the child psychoanalyst, the child's emotionally driven and nonsensical talk is the human's highest form of communication. And yet literacy scholars continue to disregard the profound role of prelinguistic expression in the child's formation of intelligible and compelling forms of language.

Psychoanalysis positions the child as a little sexual innovator of language. Observing psychoanalysis's first child analysand, "Little Hans," Freud (1909) situated the child's use of language in erotic ties to his primary caregivers. In his analysis of Hans's phobia of horses, Freud discovered that he narrated Oedipal attachments to his parents through constant references to his penis, the "widdler," and to his fears. The fictions he created to articulate his phobia consisted of a complex featuring of all three characters: horse, widdler, and parents.

Child analysis alerts us to the profound significance of psychical material residing in the innermost recesses of the human mind. Revising Freud's cases of children in light of her observations on infantile emotional expressions, Klein charted out the symbolic functioning of the child's mind. She found that the child, incredibly, innovates herself through symbolic and nonsymbolic forms of language. Analysts could gain a sense of the child's internal innovations in their engagement of the child's nonverbal and verbal expressions.

Symbolization is the term Klein uses to characterize the child's attempt to put words to a felt existence. Klein first came to her position that symbols stood in for the child's archaic fantasies when analyzing her young patient Dick. Viewing their child as severely delayed in his capacities for intelligible communication, Dick's parents sought consultation and cure from Klein. Klein concurred with the parents' finding that Dick was regressed in language development. She determined that Dick was operating at an age of development typical to the level of a child of fifteen to eighteen months. In her detailed documentation of the case of Dick, Klein notes:

> With the exception of one particular interest, to which I will return presently, he had almost no interests, did not play, and had no contact with his environment. For the most part he simply strung sounds together in a meaningless way, and constantly repeated certain noises. When he did speak he generally used his meager vocabulary incorrectly. But it was not only that he was unable to make himself intelligible: he had no wish to do so. (Klein 1930, 221)

Having determined that the child was suffering inhibition and atypical affect regulation, Klein attempted "to gain access to his unconscious by getting into contact with such rudiments of phantasy-life and symbol-formation as he displayed" (ibid., 227). She traced the rudiments of phantasy life back to an infantile conflict Dick expressed in the few words he articulated. In infancy, phantasy consists of warring mental impressions of reality that the baby sensationally experiences of an other. This incredible mental capacity to visually image the other's lived reality evolves into its symbolic forms as the child grows.

Klein closely attended to the felt experience behind Dick's "meager" and "incorrectly used words," and particularly to the force of somatic and behavioral expression by which these words reached others. She found that his muted capacity for communication had taken root in his trouble in making attachments with his primary caregivers.

To find a way to reach the unaffected child, Klein put to sustained use the one object-word holding Dick's interest captive: *train* (1930, 223). Using interpretive language and play, Klein summoned Dick's feelings for his parents to his work with the train. Following his play with his toy trains, she named the trains "daddy train" and "Dick train." She also named his mother "the station" (ibid., 225). Using her imaginative play between the daddy and Dick trains and the mommy station, Klein transferred Dick's train play to his efforts to symbolize his relationship with his caregivers. Klein used the symbol "train" to arouse Dick's ambivalent feelings about his parents. Enraptured by Klein's Oedipal train wreck imagery Dick found a place to express his anxiety and aggression. As Klein engaged his affects, Dick slowly became more responsive to others.

At Klein's suggestion, Dick began to use the train beyond its literal meaning as a toy of transport: train became the vehicle that brought him somewhat violently into and away from his primary caregivers. Through the invisible libidinal meanings that Klein and Dick attached to the train, the train exceeded its signification as a plaything with a long history in the world of child's play and toys. Train became a vehicle for Dick's internal world's expression, the means by which he could literally move to and from an emotional disturbance with his parents.

From her inside reading of the child's fragmented articulations, Klein claims, "symbolism is the foundation of all sublimation and of every talent, since it is by way of symbolic equation that things, activities and interests become the subject of libidinal phantasies" (1930, 220). By this, Klein meant that every effort a person makes to verbally and textually communicate with others is produced through a near-invisible and unimaginable process of sublimating our desires for them. We transfer a felt sense of objects into symbols or words. Hannah Segal adds: "Symbols are needed not only in communication with the external world, but also in internal communication" (Segal 1957, 396). The free associating movement of internal communication, or talking inside oneself to oneself and (m)other, is gravely overlooked in dominant practices of literacy. The child's intracommunication can provide rich pedagogical insight into each child's unique developmental process. In her work with children, Klein repeatedly demonstrates intracommunication as providing the basis for the child's capacity to externally communicate. Children silently talk to themselves, inanimate objects, and others inside themselves to express outwardly their thoughts and ideas. This activity of inside communication with (m)other uncannily resembles our inner engagement with text. In reading a novel we also grapple silently with our thoughts to gain a sense of what the other's communication holds for our own existence.

When Klein gave children words it was to support them to develop an in-mind communication with their inner worlds. Klein saw a futility in giving children words to put an end to bad feelings as if the word could silence those feelings and make them go away. Rather than ask children to use their words, she felt, the adult might offer the child words that support her inner life. The adult's careful and painstaking effort to approximate the child's feelings supports the child to build a repertoire of words to express herself to others. If symbols are resisted in the inside world they cannot be experimentally engaged and tested out by the child with others. In this silent space of phantasy the child gains the internal resources to embark on and contemplate the immense risk of saying something about her self to others.

Klein's insights on symbolization might generate a pedagogy of literacy that stretches across the life span of psychosocial development. At stake in this pedagogy is an understanding of language as relentlessly subject to intra production as it carried to the surface of social interaction. A person's fraught capacity to transform her psychical apprehension of the symbol to the symbol proper is an enormous emotional accomplishment. Literacy, then, is critical to the health of the child's intellectual *and* emotional development. If in traditional education we hold the view that literacy operates as cognition, Klein implies that literacy is always a felt labor of the meaning of words, an emotional searching of untold meanings contained by a word. The object always remains slightly beyond the grasp of language and, for Klein, we are constantly grappling with the significance of symbols—we are constantly learning how read and reread the symbols that represent our self and the meanings that house our lives. For example, it can and does take a lifetime to match the feeling of loneliness with one's actual reception by others and the world. Literally grasping the word *loneliness* does not provide one with instant relief from the experience nor does it master one's sense of the concept and the significance it holds for one's existence (Britzman 2003). Klein's theory of symbolization alerts us to the folly of thinking that our means and modes of communication can relieve us from the existential suffering associated with the demand to communicate our inchoate insides intelligibly to others. We gain sympathy for this infantile condition of being helpless, vulnerable, and sensate through our novel inventions of language and through our generative readings and representations of the world and others. Literacy, then, is of existential significance that corresponds to personality development at each stage of our becoming. Following the wavering lines of our efforts to symbolize is key to a literacy that supports the more unbearable and unthinkable aspects of being human. Literature, I suggest, taps into this fragile process and makes examinable the curious inner life of literacy.

Literature: Tapping into the Inner Life of Literacy

Scholars and writers of educational and literary studies often cite and use literature to represent elusive processes of learning. Cognitive and positivistic sociological studies tend to theorize learning as a transparent and logical process. In contrast, literature, in particular, is insightful for representing learning as a deeply intra- and intersubjective psychical, aesthetic, and social activity. Literary representations offer educational scholars other ways to conceptualize and represent micro-qualitiative processes of learning. Britzman further notes that engaging particular reading practices with literature provokes scholars, teachers and students to "[think] beyond one's means" (Britzman 1995, 163).

The bind between the literary arts and education is at the heart of curriculum studies and literary pedagogy (Britzman 2009a; Crichlow and McCarthy 1995; Eppert 2000; Farley 2012; Gilbert 2004; Greene 1995; Grumet 1988; McCarthy and Dimitriadis 2000; Mishra Tarc 2009; Robertson 1999; Simon 2005). Scholars in these fields show the kinship between educational and literary studies to be somewhat incestuous. Aspects of literary form and genre intermingle with the qualitative constructions of educational research (Britzman 2006b; Denzin and Lincoln 2000; Mishra Tarc 2011; Sumara 2002). And literature loves to engage educational ideas and experience (Coleman 2009; Greene 1995; Robertson and Radford 2009; Robertson 2001). Narrative is the dominant representation of educational experiences. The popular Bildungsroman of literature dedicates an entire genre to subject-formation as education (Rousseau 1979; Eppert 2000). Various missionary or emancipatory educational narratives often depend on literary language to give emotional power to their cause (Britzman and Pitt 1996). Teachers depend on narratives to represent and analyze their pedagogical practices (Felman and Laub 1992; Farley 2012; Lewkovich 2012; Mishra Tarc 2011). Literary artists use dominant conceptions of educational processes and discourses to represent character growth and regression in their novels (Burroughs 1939; Coetzee 2003; Morrison 1988). Conflict within and between characters is often represented in terms of learning and nonlearning (Coetzee 1986; Gaines 1993; Schlink 1997). Writers also write about language education gained through their attention to their craft, to their symbolizing processes producing literary production (Gunew 2001; Dunlop 2000; Leggo 2012; Rushdie 2005). And yet, despite deep pedagogical bonds between literacy and literary production, we have yet to fully mine the epistemological relations held by the positions of novelist, teacher, reader, and the literary text.

Recent interventions by "new" or "multiple" literacy theorists dramatically open up traditional conceptions of literacy (Freebody and Luke 1990; Gee 2004; Kellner 2004; Kendrick 2011; Street 2005). Douglas Kellner, for example, stresses the need for educationalists to broaden existing conceptions of literacy to foster critical reading and writing of media and information technologies. He writes:

> The term "multiple literacies" points to the many different kinds of always proliferating literacies needed to access, interpret, criticize, and participate in the emergent multimedia culture and society. The key root here is the "multiple," the proliferation of media and forms that demand a multiplicity of competencies, skills and abilities to access, interact, and help construct a new semiotic terrain. Multiple literacies involve reading across varied and hybrid semiotic fields and being able to critically and hermeneutically process print, graphics, moving images and sounds. (Kellner 2004, 23)

These expanded notions of literacy do bring wider possibilities to the field. And yet, as with traditional scholars of literacy, these conceptions are limited to the domain of the self-aware, speaking subject. I argue that the social precedes the child's attempts to speak, analyze text, or engage with new media. The social begins with the preverbal child in the arms of the socialized mother. Subject to time and place, the mother is the infant's first experience of social life. Conceptions of literacy continue to fail to view the social as initiated by the presymbolic internal world of the infant and overlook the significance of the infant-mother relation in language development.

In dominant theories of literacy, new and old, the learner is presumed to be mastermind and manipulator of language. The self is the sole producer of one's capacity to think, speak, and write. In a literacy of the Other, one's capacity to think, speak, and write is co-constructed where the child's capacity for language is highly dependent on how she psychically enters into and is subject to language at birth. Literacy is dependent on social ties, because the child cannot learn to speak without mother. In most theories of literacy, consideration of the child's inner life and social engagements in a discursively constructed world—the presymbolic conditions of becoming a literate subject—are curiously absent. Cummings et al. note:

> Affect, identity, respect, and human relationships: These constructs have not been evident in the radical education reforms ushered in by NCLB [No Child Left Behind], which supposedly are based on scientific research. (Cummings et al. 2005, 39)

As these researchers find, constructs accounting for the affective dimensions of literacy resist many scientific measures and instrumental practice. As a result intrasubjective dimensions of language learning continue to fall outside the domain of dominant theories and practices of literacy.

Even as new conceptions of literacy acknowledge the role literacy plays in subject formation, constructs such as affect are viewed as *effects* of literacy and schooling rather than attributed to the experience of being born to a mother who imbues the child with the meanings of words. The child's push to symbolic mastery through literacy is privileged over the infantile means through which she enters into language (Lyotard 1991). In stark contrast to dominant theories, Klein situates the conditions for literacy in the child's affect-driven compulsion to communicate her existence to mother. Literacy in this view is not mastery of the word but attributed to one's passionate attempts to seek out of words meanings that communicate to (m)other one's felt sense of the external world.

In her groundbreaking study, *Bitter Milk* (1988), Madeline Grumet finds that greatly undermined in educational theory is the role the mother plays in developing the child's capacities to symbolize. In response to the continued refusal of educational communities to take seriously Grumet's placement of the maternal in scenes of schooling, Kathleen Casey writes:

> The lack of consensus on the significance of the maternal in education is very conspicuous, both in the public forum and in academia. An examination of contemporary discourse on the subject reveals responses ranging from complete rejection (often in the form of omission) to ambivalence, celebration, and radical reconstruction, depending upon who is speaking. (Casey 1990, 317)

As Casey and other scholars suggest, the role of maternity in the education of children continues to be disengaged in mainstream studies of literacy, literary theory, curriculum, and pedagogy (Davies 1993; Grumet 1988; Walkerdine 1988; Springgay and Freedman 2012).

In contrast to maternal disengagement in educational scholarship and practice, maternity is a serious site of analytic inquiry in the archive of child psychoanalysis. Child analysts present the maternal relation as a profound and discursively formed psychosocial bond the child experiences with herself and her first caregivers. Departing from, at times, overdetermined and highly gendered notions of motherhood, child analyst Donald Winnicott (1960) suggests that the mother holds and bears witness to the child's infancy, a time that is fleeting and forgettable and, at times, deeply hated by all. Lost quickly to consciousness, infancy remains stirring in our symbolic efforts to say anything at all about the world in which we live.

Psychoanalysis also acknowledges the profound significance of narrative in the generation, formation, and sustenance of infancy and human existence. Freud cited the Oedipal story as foundational to human bonds and to the child's subject formation. Positioning the child as a tiny, greedy, envious being caught helplessly between competing desires for mother and father, Freud began to theorize the complicated psychical plot line of fundamental attachments through which the child is storied to "know thy self." He also shows how knowing thy self can go terribly wrong when the child makes the accident of taking the given narrative for the truth of the self. The technique of analysis relies on narrating and renarrating chronicles of existence through creative interpretations that can relieve a self entrenched in a story ripe for mistaken, unhappy endings. "Psychoanalytic theory," writes

Adam Phillips, is simply "a set of stories about how we can nourish ourselves to keep faith with our belief in nourishment, our desire for desire" (1999, 20). Narrative sustains human belief and desire and brings meaning to our lives.

While micro in scope, psychoanalysis also generates critical insight into macrosocial processes of colonization and subject-formation. Postcolonial scholars such as Homi Bhabha recognize that psychical scrutiny is critical to any project seeking to understand the relationship between the formation of subjectivity, literacy, literature, and colonization. Bhabha suggests: "[P]rivileging the psychic dimension . . . not only changes what we understand by a *political* demand but transforms the very means by which we recognize and identify its *human agency*" (Bhabha 1994, 42). In his work Bhabha reminds readers not to overlook the psychical dimensions of human thought and representation that construct dominant imaginaries of human life and coexistence. Colonial and other experiences of oppression are warped repetitions of the repressed and unconscious components of human behavior and interaction that cannot be silenced through consciousness raising. Instead, he suggests, our literacy and education might reckon with unbearable colonial processes that find their roots in the modern human family story, processes of human becoming that both sustain and injure human development and relation.

In education, we might afford more scholarly attention to the infant's first experiences with the mother's readings of her existence. These first, "colonizing" exchanges of attachment instantiate the baby's subjectivity at birth and her subsequent subject formation. Those who do speak of literacy's colonizing force do so in the secondary and adult context of social oppression. Spivak insists that literacy can have transformative and dehumanizing effects on the subject in-becoming. Spivak particularly cites English literacy with accompanying literary narratives as an educational tool that the British used to forge a "cultural and epistemic transformation" of colonial subjects (1992, 276). English literacy and literature, Spivak claims, produced the desired colonial effect of slowly changing elite Indians into Englishmen in the colonies.

> Indeed, literature might be the best complement to ideological transformation. The successful reader learns to identify implicitly with the value system figured forth by literature through learning to manipulate the figures, rather than through (or in addition to) working out the argument

> explicitly and literally, with a view to reasonable consent. Literature buys your assent in an almost clandestine way and therefore it is an excellent instrument for a slow transformation of the mind. For good or ill. As medicine or as poison, perhaps always a bit of both. The teacher must negotiate and make visible what is merely clandestine. (Spivak 1992, 278)

Drawing links between the manipulation of figures, meaning making, and aesthetic experiences, Spivak argues that through the process of *learning to read,* often uncritically, readers unwittingly internalize and take on forms of subjectivity represented in literature. Here, Spivak focuses on the more didactic aspects of engaging with literature and the specific case of a colonizing English. Yet, Derrida (1976a) suggests that any form of literacy inserts the learner into an ontological narrative of which she becomes subject. Language provides us with our first "colonial" education as it forms the thoughts and desires of the child in the process of becoming a literate subject. Part of that symbolic process involves inserting the child into ontological narratives to which she becomes helplessly attached. Derrida (1998) insists our literacy is always already colonizing the tiny human into the discursive regimes of social life. Literacy is so powerful because it rests on an ontological narrative that is familial and basic to the child's membership in social life.

To understand the humanizing fictions given by English literacy, it might be prudent to learn to take the literary arts seriously in our claims to empirical realities. At the same time, any attempt to privilege literature or narrative in projects of justice cannot ignore the immense role that literature plays in advancing the more violating imperatives of global (colonialist) education (Willinsky 1991, 1998). The power of English literacy to reform the hearts and minds of a global subject is archived in documented colonial letters and literature. This history should alert us to the power of literacy and its accompanying narratives in the formation of human thought and life. If the colonizers used English to make Englishmen out of native populations, so can educators orient global English and world literature to conduct a deliberating and just renewal of human thought, action, and life. Reclaiming reading and writing for its aesthetic, social, and pedagogical possibilities is so necessary in a time when current literacy practices seem helplessly sutured to the imperatives of market rationalities under global capitalism. Perhaps, now is this time "to reclaim the role of teaching literature as training the imagination—the great inbuilt instrument of othering" (Spivak 2003, 13). In this project, educators might reorient literacy as the process by which we might learn to become differently human. Conceiving literacy as dependent on the primary psychical processes by which we make meaning of the world and others, we can establish an altered relation with language and each other.

Psychoanalytic Reading, Word Work, and the Late Modernist Novel

In her review of Kafka's works for children for the *New Yorker*, Kelsey Osgood suggests that his works "can be best confronted by children, who have that empyrean way of digesting the surreal and decoding symbols, who are braver, in their innocent beliefs, than we can ever be." With this claim, Osgood also unwittingly describes the word work of the literary artist. The novelist also has an "empyrean way of digesting the surreal and decoding symbols." In their invention of incredible works with magical appeal, novelists come to their craft as the infant comes into language: searching for untold meanings cathected in ordinary words they receive from others. As with children, novelists are moved to communicate untold felt knowledge to others lodged in a unique inner life. The novel's capacity to move a reader to joy, to tears, to thinking, and sometimes to change, attests to the literary artist's capacity for "sublime word work" (Crichlow and McCarthy 1995, 206).

The three novels discussed in the chapters to follow provide fictional depictions of literacy that corresponds with my position on literacy as internally produced. I select these texts for the novelist's intentional and inadvertent depiction of psychical processes of literacy. Each author provides an experience of literacy through the reader's engagement with the novel's formal and aesthetic operation. In each novel a link is made between literacy as intracommunication, subject formation, and narrative forms of human existence. Each novelist recognizes the seductive force of narrative in the mind and life of the person. And because the authors are attuned to the modernist subject's ontological and social attachments to particular narratives of the human and human existence, these novels have universal and global implications.

The novelists of these books have a strong sense of how it is we existentially enter into language from the inside of our existence out. As John Felstiner (2001) has said of Holocaust survivor and poet

Paul Celan: some writers go to the recesses of language where reside unthinkable aspects of human existence. Or as Celan says himself, the writer "goes with his very being to language, stricken by and seeking reality" (Celan 2001, 396). In all three novels unconscious and stated forms of existentially demeaning discourse collide. Each novel can be seen as a struggle to communicate unbearable aspects of lived reality to another through the creative medium of re-symbolized language.

I characterize my readings of these novels as psychoanalytic, hinged on the inner processes of symbolization elicited by reader and the writer. In each novel, ontological problems arise in the delivery and exchange of existential meaning. Coetzee and Morrison also mine the infinite potential of language, thus engaging the reader in counterhabituated forms of literacy in the process of engaging their literature. It is this latter feature that makes their novels more than literary innovations: these novels are innovations of social, pedagogical, and political thought.

I adopt from Klein a form of internal reading to engage these novels. Klein approached the child's expressions of play using "the method Freud has evolved for unraveling dreams. . . . Symbolism is only a part of it; if we want rightly to comprehend children's play . . . we must take into account not only the symbolism which often appears so clearly in their games, but also the means of representation and the mechanisms employed in dream-work" (Klein 1926, 134). I bring Klein's approach to reading the means and mechanisms of children's expressions to my reading of these novels. I engage the novelist's craft as a form of symbolized dream work and reach behind words to gain a sense of the author's meaning. The novel becomes a holder of the writer's fraught effort to communicate meaning and the reader's labored efforts to make meaning through limited frames of reference. Reading some books resembles our infancy when we are stuck in a phantastic dream state and made to take in the reality of (m)other on the basis of feeling. Entering the fantastic space of the novel we are also anxious to make sense of the other's communication rendered by aesthetically delivered meaning. "Reading," writes Britzman, "leans on this archaic constellation of anxiety, for we actually need to project into the text, tear it apart before it retaliates, and then put it together through our 'reparative' reading" (Britzman 2009a, 49). Reading relies on one's sustained engagement with the novel's psychical means and aesthetic mechanisms of representation. Reading, we commune with the author's word work in her effort to make untold meanings known. A psychoanalytic reading wavers along the formal and aesthetic operations of the novel as the other's words compel and animate the reader's emotional response.

Reading operates by processes of development that we have already experienced, as infants, as children, as adolescents, and as adults. When we read new content we are sustained by older, invisible experiences of how it is we learned to read. The dreamwork quality of our experience of a novel is a hallmark of transference. Some novels stir in us an inchoate experience that taps into our earliest "memories in feelings" (Klein 1961, 136).

Reading three novels for the psychical dynamics they present to readers, I will examine how the literary returns us to our infancy, when oral and anal phases reigned supreme, where we are put upon to take in and put out our sense of this world and others. Following the formal and aesthetic operation of these novels, I engage the means and mechanisms of representation used by the novelists. I do not intend to provide the true or correct interpretation of the texts. My readings stage a communion between the aesthetic labor of the author's symbolization and the reader's efforts to interpret. In this imaginative space I recount, for the reader's consideration, interpretations of the existential significance of literacy as depicted by each novel. With this form of fictive reading, I will suggest that literature invites us to reconsider what it means to be literate as our work "of belonging to others and a second chance" to find and give significance to our humanity (Britzman 2009a, 59).

In the pages to follow, I read three novels as the enactment of the adult writer's word work, transference, and expressions of a sense of the world that exceeds the procedural and clear language of law, education, and sociality. Language provides the means by which the child and the artist can both fictionally invent and destroy her forms of life, her others, her ideas, and her world. When we read novels, we are gifted with words for emotional content that seem oddly familiar. The words constructing a fictional character's life can resound with our experience of the world. Novels that affect us temporarily and silently tap into our innermost emotional selves give us hints and suggestions for how to feel, think, and live the world anew. This special kinship between literacy, literature, and pedagogy is not simply a matter of comprehension, education, or entertainment. Literature constantly reminds us that words do not give us certain access to communication. Some novels, particularly those whose meanings are not made instantly available, return us to our infancy, when we struggled to find meaning without being able to communicate directly with our mother. Other novels remind us of our dreams, shifting and shaking with visual imagery, with the potential and propensity to create our most spectacular and dangerous thinking. And as with the infant with no recourse to the mother to support her meaning-making process, the novel can offer us words with no definitive direction for how to read. In these novels we dig deep to feel out aesthetically rendered meaning given to us in the novelist's cryptic, inhibited, or barred forms of communication. In this sense, the formal and aesthetic operation of some literature supports us pedagogically to relearn our methods for reading our (m)other. Literature provides us with a second chance to gain meaning about an existence that is constantly under review, revision, and renewal. Reading of ourselves in literature we can learn how to use literacy to think and story anew our lives and the lives of others.

3

Projecting Humanity

Tarzan of the Apes Learns to Read and Write

In Edgar Rice Burroughs's classic novel, *The Adventures of Lord Greystoke: Tarzan of the Apes*, Tarzan learns to read and write. The ape-man's ascent to human status is attributed to an innate cognitive achievement: English literacy. Orphaned at birth and left to the mercy of apes, the ape-child learns to read and write in English without the support of another. By virtue of the hardwiring of the human mind, the ape-child's literacy is instrumentally and incrementally accomplished. As Tarzan the ape becomes literate he becomes progressively human. He learns of his human status as he learns to name and spell: "He was a M-A-N, they were A-P-E-S. . . . From then on his progress was rapid" (Burroughs 1939, 57). As with many modern educational projects, in this novel, English literacy structures the main ontic narrative accounting for Tarzan's rapid transformation from his formative ape existence into the world of humans. Becoming literate is the pivotal moment marking Tarzan's ascension from the apes. Literacy *literally* makes Tarzan a man.

Written in 1912, the global and popular appeal of *Tarzan of the Apes* continues to this day. From its initial publication, Tarzan has been told, retold, and translated into multiple formats including: book sequels, films, theatre productions, and graphic novels. Children eagerly embrace the animated film with accompanying Disney merchandise. Richard Corliss's (1999) review of the Broadway production of Tarzan is enthusiastically titled "Him Tarzan, Him Great." Through its mass, worldwide appeal, the metaphysical assumptions embedded in the modernist novel have made their way into the minds and bodies of millions of learners. Along with popularizing American and European representations of manifest destiny and conquest, Tarzan also serves well dominant, and now global, conceptions of literacy in and as English.

Despite a fantastic premise of a self-taught ape-man, the plight of Tarzan is beloved to millions of readers. The novel's affective appeal is secured through the modern schooling experience of audiences: readers recognize themselves in Tarzan's pathos as an ape that overcomes his primal conditions through an enlightenment afforded by literacy education. They readily identify with Tarzan's formulaic process for literacy. And they identify with Tarzan's transformation via literacy from animal to human states. This narrative of literacy's transformative potential continues to ground literacy pedagogy and practice today.

Tarzan is set on a fictional African island. The parents of Tarzan, Lord and Lady Greystoke, are assigned to work in Africa by the British Colonial Office. The baby Greystoke is born on the island. His mother dies from the trauma of being attacked by the apes. Kerchuk, one of the alpha male apes, kills Lord Greystoke, leaving the baby orphaned. Kala the ape mother, having recently suffered the loss of her own child, rescues and adopts the baby, whom she renames Tarzan.

Along the razor thin line of a colonial plot, the story painstakingly documents Tarzan's history of literacy as he grows from an ape to a man. In his formative years Tarzan learns both the language of the apes and that of Englishmen. Happening on his uncle's books, and with no teacher, his human brain enables him to decode and comprehend text. Apropos to the modern colonial moment in which Burroughs wrote, Tarzan's primary and secondary processes of language development are set radically apart. Tarzan learns to speak ape from his ape mother and teaches himself English. Burroughs presents Tarzan's incredible capacity to conquer English as a natural consequence of his human mind possessed with higher-order thinking. In both cases, English literacy is intrinsic to Tarzan's human development. The ape language renders Tarzan savage, unintelligible, and dumb. English, in stark contrast, affords Tarzan civility, intelligence, and access to membership in English society.

Gore Vidal (2008) characterizes Tarzan as a "daydream figure." He suggests that such figures allow "men and boys" to materialize their fantasies of human omnipotence and power in social facts and fiction.

Burroughs's depiction of the fantastic ape-man depends on modern daydreams of literacy's power to transform the pathetic and illiterate child to a rational and literate human state. To make this fabulously literate construction of man, Burroughs makes conceptual leaps and takes literary license with the facts of the ape-child's literacy, which nonetheless seems real and believable.

In his incredible depiction of the ape-man who becomes a self-taught Englishman, Burroughs uses the genre of realism and an incremental and self-made version of literacy to give readers a seemingly credible yet completely untenable tale of one man's experience of literacy. The version is credible because it rests on a metaphysical notion of literacy as given to the human with a cognitively superior and self-contained mind. This notion is untenable because in reality no human child left orphaned in the jungle to the care of apes would survive, let alone learn to speak both the ape language and English. Although he has little social context with which to learn English as a person who lives among apes and speaks ape language, he is portrayed as magically given to English. As he naturally learns to decode words, upon viewing the words *man, boy,* and *ape,* he, incredibly, knows he is a human and the apes are "Other."

This untenable yet believable narrative of literacy is reinforced as Burroughs strategically introduces genetic dispositions to further convince the reader of the possibility of Tarzan's natural capacity for literacy. We learn that Tarzan's capacity for literacy is "endowed by inheritance with more than ordinary reasoning powers" (Burroughs 1939, 57). Tarzan's ontic dispositions, by virtue of possessing a human and thus superior mind, are designed to appeal to the reader's educated sense of the human and of self. With some pleasure, the reader identifies with the higher form of existence exhibited by the literate Tarzan while disassociating herself from his first savage, illiterate ape existence.

The story of Tarzan's literacy is a fictional tale, and yet, a version of this pseudo-scientific narrative of literacy continues to inform the idea of human advancement through education in modern times. Educators still firmly stand behind the dream of the "transformative" power of literacy as the major teleology of education. UNESCO's global initiative "Education for All," to give one highly cited example, links literacy to one's quality of life as indicated by their sixth educational goal: "improving all aspects of the quality of education and ensuring excellence of all so that recognized and measurable learning outcomes are achieved by all, especially in literacy, numeracy and essential life skills" (UNESCO 2000, 8). Literacy cannot be divorced from a conception of what it means to be human, to "essential life skills" even though, in a postcolonial time, the contested category of human is split apart and reeling. As with the novel that constructs its premise of literacy in the form of a highly literate English man, the idea of human is continually at play in the modern and global project of education.

Claiming to respond to the needs of the "whole and every child," as with UNESCO, teachers also unwittingly fix the child's existence to pervasive ontological notions of the human through the practice of literacy. Even before her arrival in the schoolyard, the child is written into humanizing imperatives of school. Schooling enacts a series of philosophical and ideological lessons through the ontological assumptions embedded in literacy education. As the child learns to spell and name, she learns that she is of man and the others of the apes. She learns of the metaphysical imperative to privilege and position her self-created self against others.

Literacy promises to take the child from an underformed to a fully formed being through education. Through literacy, the infant learns proper names designed to transform her sentient existence from an illiterate inhuman into a fully literate adult human (Lyotard 1991). *Tarzan* reinforces this idea by positing "man" as the person who names the apes and others: "[M]an *alone* and *before* woman . . . gives their names, his names, to the animals" (Derrida 2002, 384). Tarzan's transformation echoes this mythic existential rendition of literacy in a form massively accessible to readers. Consenting to the fantastic premise put forth by the novel—that the name and acquiring the name *human* is a literate achievement—readers assume and uphold literacy as they enact it to follow the plotline. For both reader and fictional character, learning to read and name deliciously confirms and consolidates one's enlightened, exalted human status.

At each step of Tarzan's English language learning, his mind is attributed with a greater capacity to think and name himself as apart from and superior to the apes. The depiction of Tarzan as a self-directed learner is also characteristic of progressive "learner-centered" literacies. The autonomous, self-enclosed learner—one book-one mind-one reader—is a privileged representation in the text. The curricular content of Tarzan's reading material poses an antagonist relation between "man" and "apes." This selective curricular content is also a representative strategy used in school to privilege some bodies over others. Tarzan's process of learning to read resembles the progressive, self-centering, personally relevant approach to reading used in current literacy practices. As in education, in the novel literacy is represented as a sovereign act of individual ability requiring the perseverance of the mind over the word, where the word corresponds with the true names of the world and others.

Eric Cheyfitz (1997) suggests the "implied" reader of this text is of a particular social class, culture, and ethnic group. I would extend this audience, suggesting, with Spivak (1992), that to form identifications with the novel, the reader must also be schooled in and passionately attached to modern doctrines of literacy. Perhaps as or more powerful than the reader's social location is her identification with the humanizing narrative of literacy. The novel sets dominant metaphysical schools of thought in motion to secure the reader's acceptance of Tarzan's impossible process of language learning. We learn these systems, as does Tarzan, through our literacy education wholly dependent on existential narratives. Children enjoy the story of Tarzan because in school they are positioned as little ape people who require the hoop-jumping steps of an instrumental literacy so they too might become a mythic figure. And as with the reader of the novel, parents and teacher-educators often require little convincing to accept various prescriptions or imperatives put forth by Burroughs for children's literacy; when teaching one remembers and reinforces in others one's often questionable experience of education. The reader's literate education, then, is critical to her acceptance of the novel's main premise of literacy.

To create a literacy of and for the self, we must contain reading, as Burroughs and educational theories of literacy do, to a mind known through one's externalized words. This externalized version of literacy promotes a self-spoken version of human communication that actively forgets the role of the other in forming our innate capacity to receive and communicate words. We need the (m)other's words to speak and make ourselves known. And so, despite Burroughs's convincing narrative of the higher powers of the self-possessing literate mind, the (m)other's haunting presence lingers in between the lines of his seemingly real and certain plot.

Rereading Tarzan

Burroughs's depiction of the apes as primitive and the human as superior is critical to his humanizing imperative for English literacy. Words such as *savage, pathetic, dark, brute* characterize Tarzan's plight as an ape. These words also signal the narrator's trouble with the human's animal states. Wishes of human omnipotence projected onto this day-dream figure inadvertently reveal the narrator's "primitive" fears and anxieties of modern man. These fears and anxieties are projected onto Tarzan's animal state and are resolved in a tale of literacy designed to rid the ape-man of his animal origins. To contain and transform the savageness of his human-animal character, Tarzan is given to English literacy.

The figure of Tarzan contains a projection of an ontic narrative of literacy that forgets the role of the animal, infant, and mother in our capacities to speak, think, and act. When reading *Tarzan*, this palpable anxiety with animal, infant, maternal, and foreign states of being circulates between the narration, the ape-man, and the reader. The novelist's hyper-identification with reified philosophical ideas of Being fortify the plotline. And yet the story does not completely hold. At various points of the novel, the narrator betrays his sympathy with the ape-man in a third person acknowledgment of Tarzan's "poor" animal plight. The narration exhibits anxiety with Tarzan, most notably, in its depictions of his dead mothers. Tellingly, thoughts of mother, baby and the difficulties of communication are fast-forwarded through Tarzan's acquisition of literacy. Literacy as given to the child by mother is one that the narrator is determined to forget.

I reread Tarzan, as a daydream figure, as a phantastic projection that emerges from Burroughs's anxieties with animal, feminine, and foreign states of being. Jonathon Lear suggests that projection identification is a phantastic process that one engages as one tries to come to terms with bad feelings experienced when sensationally grappling with the self's ambivalent relation to others. In infancy the baby makes projective identification to feel out her anxious relation to the mother. This feeling out of mother finds its basis in the baby's mental impressions of the mother's capacity to give care and respond to the baby's need (Britzman 2009b). When the mother fails to meet the baby's need, the baby experiences the mother as bad and vice versa. In a sense the infantile expressions exhibit the baby's mental gesture to put loved and hated parts of herself into her mother. Other infantile expressions exhibit confirmation of those parts in the mother's response to her (Klein 1946). Through a psychical process of finding and making identification through the projection of feeling, the baby develops internal resources that support her to make attachment to the mother. Lear

(2002) insists that this process of attachment is critical to learning and self-other relations and requires us to delve into its psychical workings:

> Of course, we know how to describe projective identification—in phantasy a person takes a piece of him/herself and projects it into another person—but what does this mean? How does it work? Our sense of the reality of projective identification is that a certain capacity of the person goes missing (Hinshelwood 1994). (590)

The hallmark of projective identification is taking a feeling one has for the other as proof of the other's character. As we grow, we retain a version of the psychical process when making identification with people and things. We take our feeling that a person is strange for the person's character. Rather than decide our feeling is strange, we decide, *she* is *strange*. We write the feeling of strangeness into a fiction that accounts for "the" truth of the person. In many encounters with foreign others we undergo a process of attributing a feeling for a person to our fiction of them. What we feel, find, or understand in the other's foreignness is our missed understanding of the person. The missing capacity of the person is then reconstructed through the self's defensive interpretations, justifications, and "proofs" of the other. Anthropological activities of colonial/educational projects are beset by the dynamics of projective identification because colonial scenes set the fictional stage of interpretation between self and unknowable others. At best, self-other interpretive encounters tend to take their basis in feeling rather than fact. At worst, they make social facts out of unreliable feeling. In self-other interpretive encounters circulate anxious feelings that manifest as our fictional findings of the other, not unlike the novelist's anxious feelings that construct the character of the fictional Tarzan.

Because literature literally involves the symbolic and aesthetic activity of depicting the other's character, literary character development is instructive for understanding the psychical workings of projective identification. Novels provide a social version of the fictive construction of the lives of others. Where literature allows the opportunity to pause, go back and read again, one's immediate feeling of the other's character is more difficult to follow. We often make instant determinations of another's personhood confirmed by larger fictive social categories and ideas of others. Stereotyping and scapegoating are examples of coarse social fictions created through the felt process of projective identification. Particularly in the extreme cases of idealized and disparaged accounts of others, the novelist's fictional construction of a character can support new understandings of the anxious and fearful internal means by which feelings construct social fictions of others.

To unravel the fantastic narrative of Tarzan, the task of the reader, Lear suggests, is to locate the "mental breaks" in Burroughs's realistic but fictive characterization of the ape, the mother, the child, and the man (Lear 2002, 592). Breaks in meaning-cohering social fictions, Lear suggests, can "open up rigid structures" of meaning (ibid., 592). He goes on to insist: "Every core unconscious phantasy is itself an implicit metaphysical theory: it provides the person whose phantasy it is with a sense of what is and what is not possible" (ibid.). Paradoxically, Lear insists, though the core phantasy is rigid, it can also provide the grounds to "be quite creative in taking in new experiences and metabolising them in terms of old structures" (ibid.). *Tarzan* provides a literary rendition of a core phantasy with an implicit metaphysical theory of Being. This theory poses the literate human as the highest state of being, a human status that takes literacy as its means to achieve the ontological axiom for human greatness. With heightened attention to conceptual breaks in the novel's depiction of literacy, readers can unravel ontological notions of existence that support our ways of being in the world but can do harm to animal, infant, and foreign others.

With Lear, Marianna Torgovnick suggests that readers examine "simple" formulations made in the novel to expose the logics constructing these formulations and to analyze the dominant, violating anxieties of "Others" they contain.

> We can appreciate now that the formulation is not so simple, that it masks a host of anxieties, uncertainties, displacements, and repressions caused by Tarzan's encounters with apes and with the human Others in the jungle—blacks and females, sometimes separately, sometimes in conjunction. Tarzan has defined himself as a "man" by his difference from the apes, from blacks, and from females, in a process that replicates the process of white male self-definition in our culture with unusual clarity. (Torgovnick 1990, 55)

Socially reconstructing Tarzan's maternal relations through gendered and racist images also works to secure the reader's hatred to an unbearable time in her development. Doing so, the narrative replicates the metaphysical theory of being guiding the modern project of literacy with incredible clarity. Traces of anxiety Burroughs projects on the figure of Tarzan are also embedded in the English imperialist project of a humanizing literacy. Reading psychoanalytically, we gain insight into the fraught relationship between the adult's humanizing wish for literacy and her projection of this wish onto the ape-child's humanity. Perhaps, after Tarzan, we can read the grand and colonial narrative of English literacy also as fiction that does hold. Unraveling the host of anxieties, identifications, and repressions circulating in breaks in the narrative is key to metabolizing the mythic self-serving construction of literacy into a literacy of the mother.

(Ape) Mother: Literacy and Mother

> High up among the branches of a mighty tree she hugged the shrieking infant to her bosom, and soon the instinct that was as dominant in this fierce female as it had been in the breast of his tender and beautiful mother—the instinct of mother love—reached out to the tiny man-child's half-formed understanding, and he became quiet.
>
> Then hunger closed the gap between them, and the son of an English lord and an English lady nursed at the breast of Kala, the great ape. (Burroughs 1939, 33)

Burroughs's anxiety with literacy's grand ontological narrative comes to the fore in his bare representation of the mother and the ape infant. Both of Tarzan's mothers appear briefly in the opening chapters of the novel. Both are killed off to advance the plot. There is no explanation for the infant's survival without his first mother and for the baby's relatively easy adoption into the animal world, by his second ape mother. The narrative also passes over Tarzan's loss of his second mother when he reenters the human world upon teaching himself to read and write. With these narrative leaps, Burroughs's fictional plotline helpfully shows some stress. The plot's fast-forward past the ape-man's infancy and death of the mother(s) to the scene of English literacy parallels the Western metaphysical jump over infantile existence on the way to Being. This jump, Lear suggests, is significant to analyzing the dynamics of anxiety that structure core ontological narratives. Burroughs's narrative-break is evident in the fractured plotline accounting for Tarzan's relation to the ape community. The glaring omission of the story of Tarzan in relation to his mothers indicates anxious and abject feelings toward female and animal others circulating in the text.

In its opening scenes, the novel enacts a primal scene of repression of the ape man, necessary to secure the tiny human's existence to a family story that starts in the middle of things rather than contemplate its suffering infancy. Rid of his animal state and mother, Tarzan's learning to read is positioned as an effect of omnipotent cognition activated in childhood as the child begins to speak of himself. Developmental language theory also depends on the plotline that rids the mother from the scene of the child's first words, attributing cognition to the child's evident speech rather than to a preverbal wordless state. In her provocative paper "The End of Reading," Peggy Kamuf reminds us:

> The common notion of reading as information-extraction sets the principles, and thus institutes the laws and the institutions through which reading practices are maintained, that is, reintroduced, reproduced, and reinforced in each new generation of readers, as we like to think of them. . . . We are taught to believe once we can read, there is no such thing as reading in this common sense, the sense we all supposedly share, sharing thus the belief that only humans read or do what we call reading. (Kamuf 2000, 11)

Kamuf insists that reading as information-extraction negates the role that the mother plays in reading. This dominant theory of reading reproduces metaphysical theories of literacy that further reproduce, according to a particular mold, the modern family of man. The plotline of *Tarzan* mirrors Kamuf's argument, where reading is an individual event rather than a practice shared with nonverbal beings. In this story of modern man, reading is the sole domain of enlightened and educated humans. Infant reading of mother has no place in Tarzan's language development. This version of reading also denigrates or ignores the apes' felt capacity to read and interpret their lived situation. With the erasures of primal scenes of reading, the novel reinforces the metaphysical idea of the human's superior reading capacity reproducing a particular kind of family of man by virtue of the practice of literacy. And according to Kamuf, these patriarchal metaphysical imperatives underlying literacy and narrating the modern family of man are perpetually and generationally reproduced in the child's learned practice of reading.

Literacy advances the plot and Tarzan into the English human race. If the apes are critical to Tarzan's survival it seems strange to completely erase the significance of his relationship with his ape mother and tongue. This move denies for the reader the role of the ape-language in Tarzan's capacity for English literacy, much the way dominant practices of English literacy deny the role of the maternal relation and mother tongue in first and second language acquisition and development (Grumet 1988). Burroughs can only keep the humanizing plot of literacy together by erasing Tarzan's ape past, and by the complete omission of the historical fact of Tarzan's ape language existence in infancy. As educators, we keep this fantastic humanizing plotline of literacy going when we deny the child's maternal beginnings and home language in our classroom teaching or when we fail to acknowledge the role of reading in the reinforcement of particular ideologies and romances of the family of man.

The novel's depiction of literacy concurs with the ontological distaste for infancy when dependency, vulnerability, and unintelligibility reign supreme. The narrator projects this hatred in the plotline by pathologizing Tarzan's "woeful" ape status while privileging his rapid entry into the human world through English literacy. Hanging in the balance of Burroughs's incredible depiction of a masterful literacy are the ape, the infant, the mother, and the foreigner.

As is the case with most developmental theory, Burroughs's killing off the mother is not new. In the modern story of the family of man, the psychical, emotional, and physical separation of child from mother initiates the child's entry into the symbolic. According to the logic of the Father, the child cannot assume a self-contained existence subject to the maternal relation. To enter into the social and the law of the father, "the loss of the mother is a biological and psychic necessity, the first step on the way to becoming autonomous" (Kristeva 1992, 27). The child must psychically and physically separate from the mother to become someone. Kristeva suggests that psychical matricide supports the child to adopt the law of the father as the governing authority of her existence. In the child's mind, where the mother once was, the father's words will be. In order for the child to become a subject (defined in Tarzan as English and male) the child abjects the embodied maternal relation to enter into the symbolic order. The child mourns the loss of the maternal relation and, through this psychical process of repairing irretrievable loss, a renewed bond with mother is formed. As if unconsciously following a theory of psychical matricide, Tarzan's entry into the symbolic is unhappily marked by the "real" death of two mothers. However, curiously, there is no trauma, psychical disturbance, or mourning process for Tarzan. Inserted into a violent and devastating break from his maternal ape and infantile existence is English literacy.

Where the "real" mother once was Burroughs invokes two narratives of maternal love. As in the novel, under the law of the symbolic, the mother is rid of personality and afforded an image that is both ideal and untenable (Kristeva 1987). However, we cannot completely forget the infantile bond that keeps us bound to thoughts of the mother. And so, as Kristeva demonstrates, we create fictions of the mother to keep her thought in mind.

Similarly, in the novel Burroughs cannot completely do away with the memory of Tarzan's mothers. He keeps both alive in his distinct depictions of each and with different ghosts of maternity. The human mother is described as tender and beautiful while the ape-mother is savage and fierce.[1] Uniting these two otherwise irreconcilable mothers is "maternal love." Maternal love sustains Tarzan on his journey to enlightenment. And yet, conveniently, the romance of the mother denies the actual presence of the mother's loss in Tarzan's acquisition of literacy. The romance of the mother, in turn, supports a narrative of literacy that forgets that without the actual presence of (m)other, the infant has no recourse to words or learning.

This active forgetting of mother, Lyotard (1991) insists, performs a desired function within Western, adult, patriarchal communities. The inability to bear the infant's inhuman condition of pathos and dependence motivates the adult to too quickly humanize the child. But this movement in the first place, Lyotard emphasizes, disavows the very unassailable qualities of humanity giving rise to the human capacity for meaning making. Addressing the inhumanness of the child with the human-making (desire-making, reason-making, culture-making) function afforded to language, the adult begins to assimilate her existence and make it fit for participation in the adult community. But what, Lyotard wonders, is the inhuman of the human? Is it "the initial misery of their childhood . . . or their capacity to acquire a 'second' nature, which, thanks to language, makes them fit to share in communal life, adult consciousness and reason?" (1991, 3).

Like all human beings, Tarzan begins as the inhuman. Given to the ape-language Tarzan emerges as a beast emitting guttural noises (cries, shrieks, grunts, and roars) and gestures (swaggering chest, pounding fists). In a gloss, Burroughs translates for the reader these sounds into a fictional language. *Tarzan*, the first word in ape-language given to the reader is translated as "white-skin."[2] Still, the ape-language cannot convey complex meanings to others: "So limited was their vocabulary that Tarzan could not even talk with them of the many truths, and the great fields of thought that his reading had opened up before his longing eyes, or make known ambitions which stirred his soul" (Burroughs 1939, 102).

As the adult community rushes the child to language, Burroughs rushes Tarzan into English. English rids him of his primitive being and his two mothers. English grants Tarzan the ability to think "great" thoughts. In stark contrast, Tarzan's first ape-language is barely mentioned but for a few dismissive sentences sprinkled in the text. The ape language is "limited in vocabulary" and, thus, in thought. And yet, even as Burroughs is able to establish the communicative primacy of the human over the inhuman there are many moments in the plot where Tarzan is confronted with conflicts between animal and human selves. These existential conflicts are presented without comment in Burroughs's story—for example, in Tarzan's severed relationship with his ape brothers or with the problem of finding love with Jane, with whom he is often unable to relate. In affective conflicts, Lyotard suggests, the human is unable to completely rid herself of her first nature and can become lost for words. If literacy teaches us to be civilized it also teaches us to violently deny a primary and primitive humanity that potentially "promises things possible" (Lyotard 1991, 3).

Where the novel, and its depiction of modern man and theories of literacy, fails to take into account the significance of infancy, Freud and child psychoanalysis take heed. Following Freud, Klein (1928) takes seriously the promise made possible by the inhuman and our infancy. Unlike other foundational theories of human development, hers locates the capacity for making sense in infancy. In infancy, before words, meaning finds form in one's internal perception or sense of objects, most notably the mother's breast. This ability to sense activates the baby's capacity to make relations between her felt perception and an indiscriminate self. Early on, the infant experiences an oppressive anxiety because she is in desperate need of the breast. At first she imagines she is the breast. As the breast actually and mentally appears and disappears she is made aware of her difference. Discerning between self and mother, she begins to relate to the breast in feelings of gratification and discomfort. Discerning, Derrida (1976a) notes, is a perception that symbolizes. Or as Spivak explains in the translator's preface to *Of Grammatology*: "What we think of as "perception" is always already an inscription" (Derrida 1976a, xl). The feelings inscribed as bad and good give the baby her first impressions of the breast. Bad feelings are split off from the good ones fragmenting the object into opposing camps—good breast and bad breast. As the object is split so is the ego. Challenging the infant's ability to manage the violence of splitting selves and objects is a later discovery; the idealized object and the hated one are actually one. She slowly begins to sense that she is making distinctions where really there are none. Upon this realization that the loved mother is really the hated mother and vice-versa, the baby is filled with feelings of grief and loss as well as guilt and shame. The baby's internal ability to work through these conflicting feelings and repair the imagined injuries caused to herself and the mother determines how easily or uneasily the ego returns itself to a state of stability (the depressive position). This process also supports the infant's capacity to make symbolic meaning of an object.

For Klein (1930), this activity of making relations to objects and others, beginning at birth, continues as the child builds up her inner world. As the child's anxiety lessens and she becomes more aware that beloved objects are outside of her, she engages in the play of substitutions; objects become replaced by symbols; symbols become replaced by words. The process is not linear, as my explication suggests. Each substitution is produced by intense psychic conflict causing the ego to regress and progress through states of instability and stability. The substitution is the child's way of addressing (replacing) psychical conflict with a conflict-free alternative. Symbolism, the mechanism for and activity of making primary meanings, develops into everyday reading and writings of the world and others. But in times of conflict, the ego regresses into infancy and one's experience of others can resemble earlier phases of development when we are lost for words and rely on feeling to make sense of the world and others.

In contrast to Klein's theory of symbolization in infancy, Burroughs textually rushes the inhuman ape baby to literacy. Literacy provides the means by which the ape baby becomes a human being. And yet, his narrative cannot fully contain his anxieties of the dependent nature of human becoming. These anxieties break through the plot in his fictional murder of Tarzan's mothers. Anxiety also reveals itself in his fleeting and ambivalent depiction of human infancy as weak and unsustainable. Kala notices that her human child is not born independent like her ape children. She decides that he is delayed: "It was nearly a year from the time the little fellow came into her possession before he would walk alone, and as for climbing—my, but how stupid he was!" (Burroughs 1939, 37). Intelligible life is a demonstrable feature of physical or mental prowess. Both views, of man and the anthropomorphic apes, render baby Tarzan as "stupid" because he is weak. Both views of "might and write" construct human infancy as pathetic and intolerable because the infant lacks visible "intelligence" and is dependent on others for his survival. In both cases Burroughs attributes the infant's lack of independence to intelligence where intelligence is conceived as mastery over one's environment or words.

For Klein (1928), these "weak" and "dumb" infantile conditions mark the very potential for literacy to be reoriented toward the other. She finds the weak, preverbal, and dependent structure of human relations in infancy to ground human thought. Our mother provides the responsive symbolizing environment without which we cannot begin to make meaning. She communicates to us in an unintelligible intelligence, a felt intelligence fundamentally based on our need of, and response to, others. We are not born with reason but with the capacity to make relations to other. This capacity to make relation supports us to take in and use the other's words to express our need to survive. And this dire need of others compels and provides the blueprint of our feelings to thought producing symbolic forms of communication.

Klein's work is often violently objected to by scholars, mothers, and clinicians alike. It was difficult for many of Klein's colleagues to accept many of her findings.[3] These reactions are very telling. I suspect that it is precisely because a normative patriarchal society cannot tolerate the infant's anxiety or her presumed animal state that mothers are forced to overdetermine and negate the infant's distress (she's hungry, she's tired, she's cranky). Klein's contemporary Joan Riviere astutely notes:

> To my mind, those who say that a baby cannot express anything might as well say a foreigner cannot speak if they can't understand him. What is required is a sufficient interest in the baby's feelings to enable one to learn his language, and once learnt, it is actually easier and simpler to report it than are the adult's complex and involved emotional processes. (in Klein et al. 1952, 20)

The depiction of baby Tarzan as the animal, helpless, illiterate, foreign infant rests on a fundamental notion of human communication as spoken and received in a language deemed intelligible to adults entrusted with her care. Klein (1952) suggests that what is required to understand infant communication is sufficient interest in and sympathy for the baby's condition: "If we are to understand the young infant, though, we need not only greater knowledge but also a full sympathy with him, based on our unconscious being in close touch to his unconscious" (94). Unsympathetic to the plight of the infant Tarzan, Burroughs's representations of English literacy bears little or no resemblance to its maternal origins depicted by Klein or even to the actual ambivalent experience of children learning to use language to communicate their existence. Instead, Burroughs's representation of the ape-language mirrors metaphysical core phantasies of existence. In this dominant narrative of literacy mothers and their babies are rid from the scene. The ape mother and his adopted ape-language are forgotten once Tarzan learns to speak, read, and write in English. Literacy is achieved solely by way of the child's possessing a superior human mind. Once literacy is achieved, the mind is given to privilege reason surpassing any former emotional or animal human state. And with reason the infant animal is transformed into the self-contained and autonomous human being that exists because it thinks and knows.

Burroughs's conception of humanizing literacy projects classist, racist, sexist, and anthropocentric representations of others onto his characterization of animals, infants, women, and racialized others. The infant has no identity except those assumed by his parents. The real mother is killed off. The ape mother is presented as functional or nonbeing rather than enabling Tarzan's language learning. The infant existence becomes synonymous with that of the ape society. The child is returned to his human Englishman status when he becomes literate. In this literate state he is afforded a human status superior to the apes and others he meets in the jungle. In this linear and progressive notion of development void of the existence of various losses and traumas, Burroughs hastily passes over critical components of infantile language development. Uncannily, Burroughs's use of the English language to civilize and dominate Tarzan mirrors the schooled way language is used instrumentally to make human the inhuman child and "Others." In his fabulous, yet unraveling, depiction of Tarzan's ascent to human status through the auspices of English literacy we can gain a sense of the ontic, colonial imperatives still driving the educational project of "literacy for all" circulating globally today.

Kamuf suggests that we reread literacy as a pedagogical practice of subject and social formation that forms, for particular means and ends, the minds, hearts, actions, and worlds of children. As teachers supporting children to learn to read and write, it can be difficult to understand literacy, a practice that we cherish and uphold so deeply, as one that can also contribute to the diminishment of the child's potential to learn to think, communicate, and be. Kamuf insists that we acknowledge the existential significance of literacy when we take seriously the literacy practices of mother.

> Reading is also thereby getting produced and maintained as site for the patriarchal, paternalistic family's reproduction of itself. The practice gets passed down, most typically, in the voice of mothers, usually mothers, reading aloud to their children. There where this ancient practice of reading aloud survives, before the child's invention of silent reading, it is the mother's voice that has been made to echo with the letters taking shape on the page. I say "has been made to" because the scene is certainly not a natural one. (Kamuf 2000, 11–12)

Reorienting literacy toward its maternal beginning requires a renewed critical and postcolonial inquiry into the role of English literacy in modern educational, colonial, and now global formations of human subjects. And perhaps in this age of information overload and the affective rise of the image, the idea of reading as a natural or desired practice can no longer hold. In this regard *Tarzan*, the novel, is more than an entertaining text for children. *Tarzan* archives the violent teleological ends of literacy to make a hyper modern English man out of the inhuman, animal infant and foreigner. Inadvertently upholding the colonial project of English literacy, Burroughs's fiction breaks open what a metaphysics of being tries to contain: the unconscious, incomprehensible, interior, other time of infancy. Highlighting a narrative break with the apes and the infants, my psychoanalytic reading demonstrates how this novel unwittingly renews the significance of the promise of humanity held in Tarzan's babbling inhuman state. In projective identifications holding the plight of the tiny ape-man to a core phantasy of higher being, Burroughs tacitly grapples in fiction with the place of the maternal relation in this depiction of literacy. Tarzan, King of the Apes, then, returns us to the profound significance of sentient states and, if we can bear a sustained engagement with the ape-man's "illiterate" first condition, to a renewal of the meanings of human as a literate practice that is given to the self from the other. In the dependent version of human being, literacy is a practice that continually revises and rewrites relations between us all. From *Tarzan* we might learn to reread literacy for the core ontological phantasy of the "daydream figure" the novel struggles to represent. Reading in between the figments of Burroughs's projection identification, we might refind the ape-person clamoring within and in dire need of the other's words to carefully nurture, story, and sustain an inhuman existence.

4

Inside Reading

J. M. Coetzee's "The Problem of Evil"

In his incredible works of fiction, J. M. Coetzee grapples with the fraught relation between literacy, language, and existence. His fictional starting point for literacy is that words continually fail us. In his novels, words often fail his characters' efforts to live well with others. It is extremely difficult, as the tragic plights of his characters suggest, to convey in words the felt motivations of human thought and action.

In his novels, Coetzee persistently figures affect or feeling as the locus of animal and human desire and communication. Coetzee's literary effort grapples with the roles of unfathomable feeling and thought in fraught human relations. Indeed, many of his novels tentatively indict thinking without a thought to feeling as responsible for the worst forms of self-other violence. Without comment, *unspeakable affect* bolsters Coetzee's aesthetic of writing in his provocative depictions of the human mind and action gripped by thoughts and feelings that run contrary to human enlightenment, morality, and civilization.

As Coetzee is loath to discuss the workings of his fiction, it is difficult to garner his real position regarding the status of affect in his works. However, in a recent statement on Animal Rights entitled "I Feel Therefore I Am," Coetzee implies that feeling is critical to a radical revision of human thought, action, and existence. Derrida has long suggested that scholars entertain the operation of affect in thinking. He finds that thinking is grounded in affective content a priori to signification (1976a, 70). Thinking/writing must rid itself of this content for the sake of textual coherence and communication. Ridding language of its affect gives us the illusion that words are Real, words really mean what they say. And yet, try as we may, we cannot completely rid thought of its affective content: a "trace" of affect remains in text, or a thinker's representation of reality (ibid., 70). Aligned with the idea that feeling drives human thought and action, in all of his novels Coetzee, quietly advances a poetics of sentient existence in the plotlines of his characters.

If Coetzee is subdued on the status of feeling in existence, his characters are not. In his novella *The Lives of Animals*, the main character, Elizabeth Costello, makes a noisy plea for sentient existence. In her treatise on the treatment and rights of the animal, Costello aggressively summons her peers and the reader to abandon philosophical principles and "open your heart and listen to what your heart says" (Coetzee 1999, 37). In the sense of Costello's heartfelt insistence, the nonhuman and subhuman exist because they feel, as we do, even if they are unable to communicate their essence in a form recognizable or acceptable to "humans." For Costello, we can survive without thinking in philosophical forms but, as is the case of the infant and other unintelligible forms of life, it is through feeling that sentient beings exist as someone in need of recognition and response.

Coetzee's fictions of feeling are curious, given that his narration of human character is often completely void of affect. Rejecting the novelist's penchant for projecting one's desire, identity, or self into one's character, he aesthetically creates, rather than discursively presents, emotionally drawn human characters. With distance from the self, I argue, he is able to imaginatively form a space of transference with his characters and to assume searing analytical insight into their internal drama. From Coetzee's stunning portrayals of terribly affected human life, the reader is given an intense and fleeting glimpse into the unconscious and not known of human behavior and interaction.

In his novels, Coetzee depicts characters as driven by principles of reality, pleasure, and death conveyed through passionate acts of often unthinkable aggression, betrayal, hatred, rivalry, enslavement, abandonment, detachment, and love. This version of the human as subject to the drives of life and death is aligned to Freud's (1920) reworking of the instincts in his later work. The void of emotion in Coetzee's narrative gives way to a novel presentation of the drives as channels of affect (Green 1999, 24). His writing of what drives feeling presses on feeling's co-opted metaphysical forms as emotion. Coetzee's novel depiction of affective life uncannily resembles the phantastic conflicts of the Kleinian infant. In subtle implosions of human folly and failure, Coetzee's character is driven by feeling, subject to feeling, and exists in feeling. Without elevating feeling above thinking, judgment, or acting, feeling is subject of and to his novel deliberations. Feelings form and steer his character's often impaired capacity for thinking, judgment, and acting in relation to others. In his belabored efforts to account for feeling, Coetzee's narrative is noncelebratory and ambivalent. The novelist's position on feeling is neither good nor bad. Instead, feeling is attributed to the human being's palatable and unpalatable productions of passion, thought, and deed. Feeling is neither constructive nor productive but an indicator of the forceful sexual and aggressive energies driving incredible and ruinous human action. Affect comes to fore of the self's more trying existential and actual crises and conflicts of life and death.

In one of Coetzee's many novel deliberations of the fragile status of feeling in human life, we meet Elizabeth Costello. In "The Problem of Evil," we do not meet Elizabeth Costello as a discrete character narrated in a story: instead, we confront the chaotic feelings that drive her to think and act. Coetzee's narrative inserts us inside the conflicted reading experience of Elizabeth Costello. This insertion gives us what we cannot observe of the other's reading: an inside view of the mind, immersed in the words of others, fully armed with barely audible devices and defenses.

Coetzee's fascinating inner depiction of reading can inform existing theories of literacy and the practice of reading. Unlike Burroughs's dominant and externalized depiction of literacy borne of superior cognition that gives rise to the human's higher consciousness, in this short story Coetzee departs from this core metaphysical phantasy of literacy. He demonstrates that reading is not only a function of the conscious and comprehending mind. Reading mostly plunges us into the unconscious where reside our difficulties with comprehension, and particularly with those representations that call into question passionate attachments to our self and others.

Where Coetzee dares to speculate, literacy and literary scholars continue to falter. In education, we have yet to take seriously the inner life of reading. Historian of reading Robert Darnton notes:

> Documents rarely show readers at work, fashioning meaning from texts, and the documents are texts themselves,

> which also require interpretation. Few of them are rich enough to provide even indirect access to the cognitive and affective elements of reading, and a few exceptional cases may not be enough for one to reconstruct the inner dimensions of that experience. (Darnton 2001, 159)

The project Darnton describes is undoubtedly challenging and is of concern to educationalists staking claim to the child's reading process solely through the auspices of external evidence. As indicated in the previous chapter, accounts of reading in its visible, knowable, and external forms are haunted by adult fears, projections, and misreadings of the unknown of the child's mind. Of this foreclosure of the inner process of reading, Darnton further remarks:

> We have not yet devised a strategy for understanding the inner process by which readers made sense of words. We do not even understand the way we read ourselves, despite the efforts of psychologists and neurologists to trace eye movements and to map the hemispheres of the brain. (ibid., 168)

Darnton's comments are pertinent to educators who base their classroom practices on evidence-based theories of the mind. And yet, he hastily looks to the "pseudo-scientists," the "psychologists and neurologists," as leading such a project of inside reading (Darnton 2001, 168). He overlooks the historical fact that, over the last century, the novelist, the literary theorist, the teacher, and the psychoanalyst have devised aesthetic and analytic strategies for engaging the inner processes by which the reader communicates and receives words. Part of this study calls for a return to literary, pedagogical, and psychoanalytic mappings of the mind because these schools of thought offer rigorous inside depictions of the mind's working. As well, these fields do not make certain claim to the workings of the unique and highly complex inner life, as often do, devastatingly and mistakenly, the "sciences" of the mind. Instead, these speculative inquiries follow the uneven and uncharted terrain of inner lives of minds in communion with the other's words. In their micro analyses of the mind's inner workings, novelists and analysts turn to fiction and not science to forge an unapologetic, nongeneralizable inquiry. My work argues that educators too might take lessons from the novel to adopt an inner view of literacy stirring in the child's mind. Fantasies, nonsense, fiction, and other emotionally invested and less accessible realities become resources guiding the teacher's literacy pedagogy from inside of the reader's magical world.

In this sense literature holds important findings on the internal workings of literacy. And it is with literature rather than eye tracking that we might place a sustained inquiry of the inner life of reading. Unlike Darnton's metaphysical understanding of the inner life as belonging to one person, in Coetzee's literary and psychoanalytic version, reading is populated by many others. Reader, writer, and their others crowd out the interior world. If consciousness gives us the effect that we are lone readers, in possession of the thoughts of our own mind, this is an illusion. Coleman (2009) describes reading as a communion of minds, as simultaneously experiencing the mind as one's own when immersed in the thoughts of another. When reading we experience a transferable quality of our mind, as our dreams, desires, memories, and experiences intermingle in thoughts of others.

Coetzee experiments with this transferable quality of mind in Costello's problem of reading: there are others living inside her experience when reading a fictional depiction of evil. Immobilized by her disturbing emotional response to a literary work, real and imagined others are brought to the surface of Costello's experience of the novel's content. A fictional account of evil indirectly references the contents of Costello's prior memory and experience of evil. It is not simply that in reading we are enraptured in our communion with the other: caught in the words of others are difficult memories of our self. Sometimes, readings bring rapture and we are transformed by the other's sublime capacity to move. Other times, reading arrives in the form of deep existential trouble in our self and with others that we might rather forget. Operating through transference, when reading, our thoughts are never our own.

Freud termed the surfacing of prior unconscious conflicts in new situations *transference*. Of transference he notes:

> They are new editions or facsimiles of the impulses and phantasies which are aroused and made conscious during the progress of the analysis; but they have this peculiarity, which is characteristic for their species, that they replace some earlier person by the person of the physician. To put it another way: a whole series of psychological experiences are revived, not as belonging to the past, but as applying to the person of the physician at the present moment. . . . These,

> then, will no longer be new editions, but revised editions. (Freud 1905, 116)

Transference is signaled in one's experience of intense feelings aroused by a person or event. Transference situations arise with an excess of infantile affect emotionally overwhelming the newly encountered person or event. Every person and event we encounter is subject to an influence of muted or noisy feelings containing old conflicts. These feelings of anger, fear, or desire highlight one's effort to comprehend the person or event. Onto the currently encountered person is transferred a total and prior situation comprised completely of feelings. Feelings deliver to the pressing scene a whole series of past psychological experiences unrelated to the present person or event. Sorting through the feelings we make new versions of old conflicts with people and things. As our situation of inner life, transference can help us gain insight into the populated internal life by which our readings are given meaning. The transference acts as both a bridge and an obstacle to meaning because our interpretation of new material uneasily relies on prior readings that unwittingly influence our subsequent efforts to make new and original accounts of people and things.

Coetzee's incredible depiction of a reader given to grief over reading brings a new *internal* dimension of inquiry to literacy and literary pedagogy. Struck with terrible feelings, animated by a literary representation of evil, Coetzee demonstrates that reading is dependent on the reader's past experience of words as they encounter new and unfamilar reading material. Reading is tied up in one's infantile frames of reference that are transferred to present interpretations of the world. As Britzman (2006b) suggests of her unsettling experience of Kazuo Ishiguro's, *Never Let Me Go*, as we read we are continually reminded of an affected life, particularly with those readings that cause existential trouble. Stuck in a novel, we can fall apart with thoughts of ourselves we cannot bear to admit.

Such is the situation of Elizabeth Costello, who finds herself broken apart by the evil she encounters on the pages of a book. Costello is undone by a fictional account of sadistic evil written by Paul West, a "real" contemporary author. And as Coetzee shows, we might do well to pay careful attention to the effect of reading on our selves. Our overwhelmed response to a novel's content gives us acute insight and experience into the significance of fiction in the story of our lives. In a sense Darnton's call for an inquiry into the inner life of reading finds a remarkable case study in Coetzee's fictional character's dramatic problem with reading evil. As we engage the chaotic ramblings of a reader's inner life, we are attuned to our inside world of reading. Our thoughts on reading are heightened as we follow the faltering lines of the inside life of a struggling reader. Coetzee's novel experience of the inner world caught in the throes of a literary text can bring us to a new understanding of reading as caught up in the recesses of emotional life and subject to the secrets residing within.

Stuck Reading

An experience in reading can leave us shaking from the outside in. Some texts get under our skin and find their way to the fragile raw material of a carefully concealed self. Novels can provoke from us intense gut reactions and irrational emotional outbursts. Some content presses our buttons. We shut the book vowing never to return. We are left at a loss. How did we let a mere book get to us? Why did we not flee when we still had a chance?

This is the case of J. M. Coetzee's fictional character Elizabeth Costello, a mother, academic, and celebrated novelist stricken to the core simply by reading a book. Costello, a key figure in three of Coetzee's works, embarks on reading a fictional depiction of atrocity. Confounding her reading is her knowledge of the actual, well-documented event of mass killing and degradation with which the book materializes. We enter the scene of Costello's reading trouble as she engages unthinkable images of atrocity in Paul West's novel *The Very Rich Hours of Count von Stauffenberg.* As she flips through the pages upon pages of sensational human on human violence she becomes overcome with terrible anxiety. She decides, "I do not want to read this" (Coetzee 2003, 178). Horrified by West's depiction of the mercenary actions of Hitler's executioners, she shuts the book. Deeply agitated with the writer's graphic depiction of human torture and extreme suffering, she wonders how anyone could imagine, let alone write, such scenes of "obscenity." Filled with revulsion, she decides that West's book is not fit to read. Moreover, she determines that representing this evil (and reading it) is immoral. *Yet,* she is unable to stop reading. Taking in West's scenes from the Shoah, despite her best judgment, "suck[s] her into a mood of bottomless dejection. *Why are you doing this to me?* she wanted to cry out as she read, to God knows whom" (ibid., 157).

West's novel afflicts Costello with palpable, unbearable feelings. Overcome by a fictional depiction of evil against others, she is "sick with the spectacle, sick with herself, sick with a world in which such things took place, until at last she pushed the book away and sat with her head in her hands" (ibid., 158). In this stuck place of interiority, Costello cannot get away from West. Riveted to Coetzee's novel, we cannot get away from Costello. Readers are literally trapped in the internal dynamics of transference narrating one reader's crisis of reading. Caught in the thick of Costello's reading breakdown the reader is put upon to sort through the internal trouble that reading makes for Costello's disintegrating sense of self. A literary representation of evil sends Costello spiraling into an uncontainable flurry of thoughts. At times, her emotional and starkly contradictory reading response disables her, the narrative, and the reader. In an intense, grief-stricken push for symbolic relief, the narrative and the reader travel rapidly along the shaky arcs of Costello's conflicting thoughts. One reads this short story through Costello's nonsense. We circle round and round Costello's mind with no explanation given for her stuck reading. With only shape-shifting feelings as a guide, the reader is lodged in Costello's conflicted mind.

The effect of reading in the inside of another's reading is strange. Gripped in a fictional character's inner strife, we can feel removed from our own minds. Character and reader are fixated by startling narrative circumstances and by the traitorous infiltration of despondent, "black thoughts" that refuse to let Costello and the reader go (Coetzee 2003, 160). Pounding in this overwhelming narrative of feeling are Costello's relentless thoughts of West. She starts to blame West for her trouble, projecting her anger aroused by the book onto the author. As she disparages the book she disparages West, a person she has never actually met. Because she deems the book immoral and giving rise to monstrous thoughts, she deems West immoral and a monster for imagining and writing such a book. She has no idea where her bad thoughts begin and decides they end with him.

It is difficult to know to whom Costello directs her thoughts. She appears to be talking to a person West only available to her in her mind. She creates fantasies about West to presence his absence. Once he is fantastically conjured in her mind, she accuses West of the unstoppable suffering the fictional "he" brings. She indicts West inside her self. She indicts his world capable of such violence. She indicts herself for reacting to a mere novel so badly. She talks to herself to talk out her bad feelings with herself, the novel, and West. And in these, imaginary conversations teeming with anger and revenge, she labors to work out her conflict with West to work him and his novel out of her mind.

Costello finds no relief from the book despite waging with it and its author internal war. Continually failed are her numerous defensive attempts to ward off the novel's distressing affect. Obsessed with West, she decides to use his book as an example in her invitational international lecture on "Witness, Silence, and Censorship" (Coetzee 2003, 160). Rather than give her "routine censorship paper," liberal in its acceptance of free thought and speech, she decides she will use West's book for a public occasion to vent (ibid.). After her encounter with "West's" evil, she concludes that some ideas should simply not exist: "She has begun to wonder whether writing what one desires, any more than reading what one desires, is in itself a good thing" (160). Strangely, her new insight devastates. The decisive position offers no consolation. She is unsure of her change and wracked with not knowing. She grows tired, despondent, and disoriented. She is unable to focus, deliberate, or reflect. She fights and fights with herself to justify and reach a sound conclusion to her changed views. But the view makes no sense to her writerly self. The view makes no sense to the reader. And yet, she clings to her rigid position without knowing why.

As the day of her talk approaches, Costello is overwrought with conflict. She begins to second-guess herself. She grows to hate her newfound position on West's novel. She grows to hate herself. She grows to hate West all over again. In the midst of her hateful thoughts, she learns that the actual West is in attendance at the conference. Faced with the real prospect of facing her imagined nemesis and the leading character in her fantasies of revenge, Costello is stricken with immense, immobilizing anxiety. The force of moral outrage she experienced while writing her conference paper instantly dissolves in fits of panic. She is sleepless and "stays up all night wrestling with the lecture" (Coetzee 2003, 164). She cuts out and slashes her paper's textual references to West and his novel. She softens her argument by removing potentially offensive passages. She berates herself for reacting so violently to a man she has never met. She is nervous about how her talk will be received by him and others. She grows heavy with doubt. And then suddenly, without warning, in the midst of these endless thoughts of herself, of West, of her lecture, of evil, and of censorship, she *remembers*:

> It was her first brush with evil. She had realized it was nothing less than that, evil, when the man's affront subsided and a steady glee in hurting her took its place. He liked hurting her, she could see it; probably liked it more than he would have liked sex. . . . Why does her mind go back to this long-past and—really—unimportant episode? The answer: because she has never revealed it to anyone, never made use of it. . . . For half a century the memory has rested inside her like an egg, an egg of stone, one that will never crack open, never give birth. She finds it good, it pleases her, this silence of hers, a silence she hopes to preserve to the grave. (ibid., 165–66)

Lodged in the kernel of Costello's relentless bouts of self-punishing thought are the affects of a traumatic rape she experienced in her youth. The memory bears down on her and breaks the narrative wide open. The memory of a rape appears like a still-frame in between her rambling thoughts. For the reader there is a moment of relief. We hope that, finally, Costello will recognize her problem. But the moment passes with no comment from Costello. Oddly, she puts the memory away. She continues on as if it never happened. The reader is left to wonder: Did something happen? There is no sign of the memory. Perhaps it is too soon. Or too late.

Britzman reminds us affect "is too encrypted with other scenes to count on understanding" (Britzman 2000, 43). Perhaps there is more to this memory than we think. Perhaps the memory has little to do with thinking.

In the middle of Costello's trouble with reading arises a memory of evil. Her failure to repress the memory of a violent rape intrudes upon her fictional reading of violence and mass degradation. The rape resounds in her reading. The memory of rape in her reading resounds in the reader.

Lyotard's (2002) revision of Freud's (1905) case of Emma provides insight into the somatic qualities that reading can labor to express. Emma came to Freud with a fear of shops after experiencing a spell of fainting in one. Freud probes her somatic response to the shop to find that Emma's fear belatedly references a childhood experience of sexual abuse at the hand of a shopkeeper. As with Costello, Emma does not remember the earlier assault. She has mostly repressed the incident. In puberty, the childhood repression fails to be kept down. Emma's fainting spell reanimates childhood affect in her youth in radically different form. What was repressed in childhood can no longer be held down in youth (Freud 1915). The silenced affect of childhood trauma morphs into communicable form in youth. "Puberty in no way creates them, as it creates only another 'reading' of an affect already there" (Lyotard 2002, 36). Similarly West's novel does not recreate the affect of abuse Costello experienced at the hands of a sadistic[1] rapist. His novel resurfaces affect in communicable form. Her memory of the rape provoked by West's (evil's) presence[2] creates "another reading of an affect already there." Affect renarrates for Costello a previous story of real evil that plagues and is plagued by West's fictional depiction of evil.

Without warning, we find the memory of abuse breaking into the narrative. Can the reader hear the significance of the new edition of Costello's trauma? Costello certainly does not. She leaves the memory of evil and continues on as if it never happened, as if it isn't there.

If the content of the memory fails to make sense, Costello *is* affected. The absent presence of affect testifies to an unspeakable yet totally felt experience of trauma. This trauma circulates in Costello's terrible feelings about West's novel. Traumatic affect lodges itself in Costello, stirring in her incapacity to read, in her incomprehension of evil and in her cognitive difficulty with West's novel. Affect rather than West's novel says something to her. Or as Lyotard simply puts it: "The affect only 'says' one thing—that it is there—but is witness neither for nor of what is there. Neither when nor where. The affect says only that it is there *if one pays attention to it*" (Lyotard 2002, 32; italics added). Affect bears unreliable witness to an unspeakable event. It says nothing, and yet all along, Coetzee's narrative pays cryptic attention to traumatic affect in Costello's trouble with reading.

Costello's reading trouble signals her unconscious response to an experience of evil surfaced only by reading and in subsequent relentless attempts to process the unthinkable content writing West's novel. This prior and unresolved conflict transfers to Costello's impaired capacity to make sense. Her past impairment afflicts her present interpretations of West's depictions of evil as "obscene," "immoral," and "excessive." Her past experience diminishes her capacity to engage and makes sense of evil, then and now. Costello's interpretations in crisis contain a trace of traumatic memory startlingly popping seemingly from nowhere out of the barrage of her self-sabotaging thoughts. This unthinkable memory bars her from reading the contents of West's novel apart from her own.

Terribly ironic is Costello's refusal to analyze her experience in relation to her reading of West's novel, given her original drive and determination to know why, in the first place, his book upsets her so. The refusal is curious, given her hysterical decision to make a transatlantic journey to confront, first, West's novel and then West himself, wrongly blamed for her mental strife. Any real or fictional capacity to think about or through evil is too tied up in Costello's actual and still partially repressed brutalizing experience of evil at the hands of another. And yet, if she seems completely unaffected by memory's vivid revelation and unable to hear and read the terrible existential content it contains, the novel resounds back to her an evil that ultimately will not be kept down. As she indicates to herself after her lecture and her bungled attempt to confront West, "something has happened" in the span between "now" and first "reading the accursed book on the lawn that Sunday morning" (Coetzee 2003, 177). She asks herself, "What was her experience? What was it that upset her so much that a year later she is still grubbing after its roots? Can she find her way back?" (ibid.). A year later, and with distance to revisit her crisis in reading, Costello continues "to grub at the roots" of her problem of reading. In the after time of a resurfaced trauma, she is longer held to the original force of disturbance experienced in the real time of reading West's book. And if Costello and the reader go back and interpret, this "thing" might hold profound insight for both. Reading, then, can take us unwillingly back to a self we thought we had left behind for good. We can refind ourselves in a book in detours made through the thoughts and words of another. And finding ourselves again in thoughts of the (m)other can contribute to our change (ibid., 160).

"I do not want to read this": Literacy's Inner Life

In *Psychoanalysis and the Scene of Reading*, Mary Jacobus conceives reading as an intensely subjective, intrapersonal activity. When reading, we travel back to internal worlds of self and other populated with transference figures collected over a lifetime. Literary works, in particular, immerse the reader in psychical processes cohering the reader's sense of the writer's text. Reading mediates an intimate, one-to-one communion between the innermost thoughts and feelings of a writer and a reader. Jacobus (1999) suggests that, more than any other symbolizing activity, reading literature allows us the temporary pain and pleasure of entering into the timeless (un)conscious thought of the other. The pain and pleasure of reading some fictional works, she suggests, reminds us of an earlier time in childhood and infancy when we struggled by any available means to take in, make sense of, and articulate our desire and need of the (un)known contents of the (m)other's existence. Communing with the other's psychical stuff, driving the emotional content of fiction and formally and aesthetically arranging some literary works, we are returned to our infancy. Here, stuck inside ourselves, we first magically learned to make sense of fleeting feeling reverberating inside and to and from the inside of mother.

Jacobus (1999) demonstrates that literary readings can find and give confirmation of the internal workings of the mind as constructed by psychoanalysis and deconstruction. As well, as Britzman (2006b) finds in her engagement with Ishiguro's existential science fiction, the spectacular thought residing in a novel can make us painfully aware of our own insides, particularly when our constructs break down beneath the weight of our difficult readings. At the moments when reading is slow and interpretations fall short of comprehension, we can find ourselves helplessly flailing for a semblance of meaning of our self and others. Britzman reveals that there is much in reading that we do not know, are not ready to know, cannot begin to know, and may never know. A certain kind of reading teaches us to bear a fragile leap of faith held by the thoughts of the self in an attempt to make relations to those of the other. As it did for Costello still grappling with the book a year later, reading profoundly affects us even if we do not wish to be affected.

Jacobus, a literary scholar, and Britzman, a scholar of education, look to Melanie Klein's study of the internal worlds of infants to think through the intricacies of one's reading development. Unlike many literacy theorists, Klein (1955) situates "reading" in the pre-Oedipal time of infancy and childhood when human beings first begin to make relations with objects. Klein (1928) theorizes the baby's need of (m)other as activating the child's innate and ordinary capacities for reading the world. In dependent, immobile infancy, first reading characterizes our fragile attempts to make sense to survive felt and threatening sensations coming at us from the world. Departing from the daydream figure of Tarzan, who is possessed of a fully developed mind, in Klein's theory of reading, without warning the mind is prone to splitting, to regression to infantile states of incomprehension. Reading, in this sense, relies as much on feeling as it does cognition and, for Klein, these processes are inseparable.

Coetzee's portrayal of Costello's reading difficulties is located in the infantile regression of a deeply affected reader. As with the baby toward the mother, the novel animates affects of hostility and dependency in Costello. Hostility and need arise from the baby's limited capacity for making sense of the mother's words and gestures. Similarly, the hostility and need for comprehension of West's novel arise from Costello's overwhelming incapacity to make sense of the novel's depiction of evil. In both cases, the infant and the reader are put upon to make sense of unfathomable feelings animated by the other's intrusion into one's mind. In the case of this reader, these affects silently yet symptomatically show themselves through her paranoid and hysterical response to a novel. In her disturbed state Costello uncontrollably wrestles with resurfacing, seemingly from nowhere, affects rudely interfering with her capacity to know what the other is saying. She is caught by and forced to contend with the transference of affect from another time and space flooding her sense of what the contents of the novel are concurrently saying to her.

Costello is reduced to childlike behaviors in her rush to know why she is so bothered by West's novel. Her trouble with the book's content spills out of her in an outburst of uncontrollable hate directed at the unknown novelist. She compulsively and repetitively babbles out rationalizations of this hatred in an internal, irrational monologue she holds with the fantasy person West. She makes various attempts to deny the novel's worth and denigrate the writer's craft. She holds great resentment toward the novel and West for giving her such grief. Desperately searching for relief from the grievance carried within, Costello begins to childishly project her feelings of the novel's "obscene, rank touch" onto West's book and to some extent him (Coetzee 2003, 159). When her hateful feelings fail to subdue Costello, she turns to a public opportunity to violently and finitely destroy the novel and tear into its author once and for all by way of a scathing, overdetermined, punishing critique.

When affect is animated in adulthood, we are faced with an infantile vulnerability calling out our need of others. This need is irrational, unreasonable, relentless, and yet, paradoxically, our pathetic need of others is critical to the self's survival. Our dire need of others presses intelligibility on a self without recourse to words and speech. Driven to survive, the infant sensationally expresses herself in affective communication designed to reach her mother. Klein (1937) finds the infant gains perspective on the affects animated by perpetually working through her strained feelings for the mother. Costello, too, through her inability to let go of West's novel, is bound to repetitively work through her straining response to his novel. At first, the novel's grip on her is too much. There seems no way for Costello or the reader to gain a handle on reading's insurmountable challenges. But residing deep down in Costello's inability to let go of the object is her great need. Costello desperately needs this novel to bring renewed meaning to her life and to gain another perspective on her disturbing reading and disturbed self.

Reading Affects

What we learn from Costello's disturbing reading disturbs. Costello herself has been unmercifully subject to a horror as unthinkable to her as those resounding off the pages of West's horrible text. Her firsthand encounter with evil, experienced in a brutal rape, is psychically called forth by traumatic affects that resurface in the pages of West's incomprehensible depiction of human atrocity. In the transference animated in herself by a prior experience and a novel, Costello psychologically engages evil in a series of intimate intratextual and intertextual events. Her reading of evil bleeds off the pages of West's novel into her memory, experience, relation with others, ideas of writing, and previous readings of traumatic history and the world.

Costello's capacity to objectively engage with the form and content of evil is experience-afflicted, and so reading falters and falls apart. As reading falls apart so does Costello. Costello is shown to suffer a reading breakdown that repeats and resembles the actual mental breakdown she suffers to survive the aftermath of a violent rape. These breakdowns in mind and memory ruin and leave in ruins her subsequent capacity to comprehend representations of evil. Costello cannot engage the fictional idea of evil, cannot understand evil, cannot master the contents of evil because her experience of it renders her helpless at the thought of evil. Meaning breaks down not because she cannot decode the words on the page but because she is barred from the novel's sealed-off content, a content that has previously threatened and thus still feels threatening to her own existence.

Costello's horrific inner suffering animated by West's depiction of suffering also revives a memory critical to her repair. Reading can take us back to our psychical injuries. These wanted or unwanted returns can lead to breakdown or relief. Perhaps, readings that bring both ruin and repair "contribute a change" to our minds and lives (Coetzee 2003, 160). A crisis in reading can lead to renewed insight. It can also lead to further inhibitions when reading. Despite traumatic memory's fleeting appearance, Costello continues to deny the impact of the rape on her impaired capacity to engage with evil. However, in spite of her will to preserve the memory in silence, she also indicates that insight garnered from West's novel alters her relation to evil. Each failed attempt to work through her problem with West's novel culminate in an exacting mental excavation of a deeply buried memory encasing a silent suffering untold for fifty years like an "egg of stone" (ibid., 165–66). Working through psychical disturbances against the unresponsive, unaffected fantasized person of Paul West, Costello is given some relief from a forgotten but incompletely repressed trauma with which she has yet to come to terms. In her case, coming to terms with her personal experience of evil is too much to ask on a first reading and even on a second or third. However, working through evil as represented by another does provide her with an opening. She herself eventually realizes that somewhere between her half-century-long grief with evil and her present facing up to the problem of evil "She has a choice" (ibid., 182). And in this reader's grief-stricken insight we feel a slight sense of release, renewal, and repair.

In a few pages of this short story, Coetzee skillfully demonstrates that reading operates on the aesthetic/affective registers of the text. The feelings that words animate and bring to the fore of one's reading are an enabling feature of cognitive processing that is yet to be explored in literacy education. Costello could decipher the words on the page but could not comprehend them. Her felt knowledge of words preceded her capacity to know. With no interpretive outlet, she projected her bad feelings onto West and his novel. These projective identifications gave her temporary relief from the psychical grip of trauma the novel unearths. However the traumatic, affected injury contained in her projections could not get her off trauma's piercing hook. Words, constructs, and reasonable thought can fail reading, as it fails both Costello and the reader, when our psychical injuries rub up against the limits of our interpretive capacities and refuse to admit what conflicts for us the novel's affect animates and holds.

Coetzee's text powerfully moves both reader and character through an aporetic experience of deferred meanings until a semblance of inner sight, in a flash of memory silently screaming its traumatic affect, pierces through the dull and obtuse surface-edge of words. As readers, with Costello, the mute force of a trauma afflicts our capacity to interpret the meaning of a fictional character's reading difficulty. The narrative drives us to feel affect before we know of the trauma residing deep inside Costello. At times this sensation—being held captive inside the other's head—can be oppressive. Reading her mind, we feel confused by Costello's internal confusion, persecuted by her persecutory feelings, distracted by her mind's many distractions. Reading feels as if we are going around and around in circles to end up nowhere and to become none the wiser. The unruly and invisible affects become the medium that steers one's faltering reading. Radically unlike the progressive narrative of conventional fiction, these affects, with their accompanying grating tones, mixed signals, and wrong directions, construct a narrative force that carries, frustrates, belabors, and defers one's reading. The reader is pushed, prodded, and pulled back and forth by the narrative and she is startled, with Costello, to learn the secret the affect-steered narrative keeps. Immersed in Costello's emotional journey, we can quickly become lost as her feelings of elation and despair rapidly fluctuate. We can also helplessly wonder: What is this novel doing to me? And we can think: maybe the formless affect driving the narrative *is* the narrator.

Costello and the reader are made to fight through the mental labyrinth of a reading in crisis and confusion. We are given few conceptual constructs and resources to penetrate the thick barrier of affect the internal world erects to fortress the self from its knowledge of an evil that it cannot bear to admit to know. Coetzee shows that with and without firm conceptual ground, past experiences can sink and survive our reading. Without the "terrible gift" of reading West's unfathomable novel, Costello might never have encountered the internal impetus to return to the repressed "something" she carefully hid inside away from others (Simon 2006, 187).

Disturbing readings make shaky attempts to penetrate layers and layers of the reader's psychical stuff. Reading for the truth of the self and other's meaning can bring news and newness to our understandings of the world (Britzman 2003). Reading as the carrier of news and newness also returns us to the internal means by which we seek repair of the harm we imagine or actually experience at the hands of others. Resurfacing affects holding deeply and partially repressed injuries to our self, reading seeks out the self's repair. In these moments, with some texts, reading can help us "find our way back" to what Melanie Klein calls "the strangeness of ourselves" (1940, 338).

Readings in crisis serve as the means by which we restore an internal world shaken by the unknown contents of traumatic grievances recorded unconsciously inside. Although it can be hard to tap into the qualities of our grief when we are in the thick of it, our troubled readings can compel us to go back to the beginning and start again. In the second-chance, after-time of novel readings, emotional responses become blueprints holding startling and original interpretations of self and others. Our second and third readings give us the opportunity to "[h]old fast to the word, then reach for the experience behind it" (Coetzee 2003, 177), to think through the disturbance that reading presents to a confronted self begging for meaning in words. Reading invites one to be uncomfortably at home with one's unthinkable thoughts of self in the words of others.

Twisting and turning along the contours of Costello's psychical ruin and repair, we can grow weary with reading. The confused text is strewn with reading stops and stalls making the reader think: *I don't want to read this*. However, the affective grip Coetzee's narrative has on the reader, the thing that keeps us going, is the novel's implication in our reading. Costello's insufferable processes of thought seem vaguely familiar and oddly comforting. One is at home and not at home in her chaotic, mood-altering non-sense. Our transference of past difficult readings onto a fictional reader's crisis is the glue. When read for its affect, Coetzee's representation of his unforgettable character takes on new meanings for reading and writing—for literacy—offering us "the opening of new signifying organizations . . . new possibilities" (Nouvet 2003, 245). The opening of new significant organizations of the self and others grounds our capacity to repair and renew our wounded and wounding self-suffering relations with others and the world.

We have not yet come to think of reading as a process by which the self and world can be made, ruined, repaired, and remade in the span of a few hours or days. Coetzee's sustained attention to his female character's churning inner life dramatizes quite starkly and remarkably one's internal world in conflict. The naked inside view of reading he gives disturbs dominant well-dressed conceptions of reading. From the novel we are left wondering *What is this thing reading?* and how, in its ordinary and formal sense, reading makes and remakes one's thinking and acting in the world.

Peggy Kamuf (2000) suggests that we need interdisciplinary resources to forge sustained inquiries into the inner life of reading. I further argue that a particular kind of engagement with literature can give readers interdisciplinary insight into reading as an interpretative practice that transforms inner social fictions into external social realities. I say a "particular kind" of reading practice of literature because I do not think we have learned to read the text imaginatively, speculatively, experimentally, tentatively for what it cannot say in words and only in feeling. Our most common way of reading is functionally, for the purpose of "comprehension." We read to contain and master the world and others. Teachers of literacy and literature can learn much about one's less ascertainable internal process of reading from engagements with novels that place one into alienating yet strangely familiar practices of reading. Some novels can return us kicking and screaming to our first readings of the world and others. When meaning breaks down we use our feelings to guide our sense of objects and things outside ourselves. Our difficulties with reading can compel us to rethink how it is we have impaired human existence with disciplined methods and practices of interpretation that fail to do justice to the infinite unfathomable qualities of sentient life (Lévinas 2003; Coetzee 1999).

Reading, Britzman reminds us, is a faltering attempt to feel out unstable meanings always already exceeding our means to gain complete understanding of knowledge and things.

> Psychoanalytic reading teaches us a lesson we already know, that we cannot let go of affected life, we are always reading between the lines, wagering meaning and deferring it. Here is where we find that our constructs fail. (Britzman 2006b, 317)

As literate subjects, we discount uncertain feeling bolstering childhood interpretations. In school we are made to favor a disciplined practice of reading reproducing illusory grand narratives upholding adult concerns. Literature can help us and our students return reading to its childhood, a time when words were few and we had to use feelings about the world and others to unravel the (m)other's surprising plot line of our affectively narrated, precarious existence. Reading, then, might teach us to bear the soft and inchoate inside of our being, as the limit to thought and the folly of believing too determinedly in hard and evidenced-based knowledge as the truth of our existence. Here, suspended disbelievingly in the timeless space of reading, we can learn of our profound affective need of the other. In this intimate, sacred space of communion we think to forget, we read to make ourselves recognizable, grievable, survivable, memorable, lovable (Coleman 2009).

A crisis in reading can alert us to the others residing in our minds. Coetzee's flawed human story of disturbing reading reminds us that reading is not only our lifelong project; reading is also our lifelong projection because language makes of us what it will as much as we forcefully will language to make us other than what we once were. Reading is a felt situation, operating in the transference of prior experience to new editions of our vexed understanding of social life. Reading is an affectively layered process, one that recalls and enacts prior injuries and achievements. Reading alerts us to a waiting world of others. Without an inner world our readings are deadened by social discourse and contents. Void of feeling, we can find ourselves unable to attach to our representations and apathetic to meaning. And, as I have shown in this chapter and extend in the next, some reading supports interpretations that can make a profound difference in the renewal of our selves, life and social life. A gift of startling literature, then, contributes a lasting change to our experiences of ourselves and the world. Reading of ourselves in a novel, we return to the human beings we were once and always meant to be—helpless creatures dependent on dreamy, felt readings, grappling with the frailty of human significance gracefully given to us through the words of others.

5

Healing Language

Beloved, Literacy, and the "Other"

Ten years after publication, Toni Morrison's *Beloved* continues to hold readers in its grip. Written on the edge of the symbolic, *Beloved* reckons with the collective and deeply suppressed trauma[1] of African American slavery. Morrison dredges up memories of "transgenerational" trauma in the lines of a fractured narrative. Given the vast array of scholarship written on the novel, *Beloved*'s literary significance is undeniable. Attending to the existential significance of Morrison's depiction of literacy, I address the important and compelling question Susan Huddleston Edgerton and millions of readers ask of the novel: How does this work leave its mark on me? (Edgerton 1995, 347).

Although many scholars make interpretations of the power, imagery, and moral message of Morrison's novels, few discuss the psychosocial implication of her writing for literacy. With *Beloved*, Morrison abruptly departs from the dominant conception of literacy as possessed by the superior mind, and as depicted in Burroughs's *Tarzan*. Where Burroughs eliminates the presence of the inhuman, "ape" infant with the humanizing imperatives of Western ontology, Morrison resuscitates the infant from the more extreme effects of these imperatives. Unlike the grand narrative of the savage child in desperate need of humanizing through English literacy, Morrison's human story of literacy acknowledges its heavy debt to primitive infancy.

Infancy, as I have argued throughout this book, grounds the language development of the becoming human. Setting the scene of literacy in the rebirth of a monstrous fully grown infant, Morrison stages an "originary," violent entry into language as potentially generative (Derrida 1976a). As readers, we feel the overwhelming experience of entering into a new language, as the infant, the slaves, and the reader are dragged through fragments of poetry flashing back the human's traumatic social history. Posing the colonial project of language education as a blunt force trauma of mind, Morrison highlights the traumatic and persistent internal effects of a community's literacy in dehumanizing schools of thought.

Returning to the world ghostly and in adult form, Beloved is locked in a strange, infantile state. Stuck in the murderous internal world, language is infused with the furious sounds and sights of the vengeance-seeking prelingual baby. Babbling out an accusation against a vicious external world, Beloved wages infantile revolt, pitting a preverbal code against dominant representations of the human and literacy. Rather than repress the presence of the infant in the novel, Morrison uses the specter of Beloved to poetically fragment the affects of mass violence haunting the infinite potential of one of millions of imagined lives impacted by the transatlantic slave trade in the Americas and the world.

Beloved, the adult-baby, manages to disturb all with her unexpected and terrifying appearance. Her infantile presence holds the reader captive to the baby's clamoring, preverbal need. As if guided by the murderous insides of the Kleinian baby, Morrison invokes language through the out-of-joint occasion of Beloved's ghostly rebirth. I attribute the difficult reading experience of the novel to Morrison's aesthetic and formal construction of an interior experience of infancy and extreme trauma waged against the excesses of history. Confounding one's reading is one's unfamiliarity with this horrific interior version of history. I would hesitate to imply that Morrison's literary renewal is deliberate, and yet, in some works, the writer's existential conflicts with personal and/or traumatic history transfer to the narrative and steer the reader's reception. Some novels, as the ones I engage in this book, shake with potential transference between writer and idea, writer and history, writer and character, writer and text, and writer and reader. The psychical exchange of inside and actual histories between real and fictional individuals who never actually meet fuel one's affective reading. Immersed in a novel, competing internal and external realities surface and reading is labored, pushing us beyond our interpretive means (Britzman 2000). Our reading strife can bear great emotional weight and bring the significance of our own lives to the forefront of the other's unfamilar narrative. In a novel, we can be made to grapple with the fragile stuff of our lives, and to reckon with our implication in the other's life and in history.

Warren Crichlow and Cameron McCarthy characterize Morrison's literary efforts as "language work, sublime 'word-work'" (1995, 206). They insist: "Literary discourse cannot be separated from material relations and social consequences"[2] (208). In this regard, Morrison's language work has immense significance for existing practices of literacy. In the final part of this book, I argue that the resignifying work enacted in Morrsion's *Beloved* brings important news of the socially reparative potential of literacy. Our careful and painstaking use of language can bring forth the unique qualities of individuals and rewrite demeaned representations of the lives of "Others." This renarration does not simply offer a counterversion of history. The creation of resigned literary and linguistic mechanisms, means and modes of representation, of what Sethe calls "rememory," writes lives of deformed others into historical account. With *Beloved*, Morrison wagers on fiction's second chance to renew fraught terms of human existence, restore the historical record, and renarrate humanity.

In its capacity for symbolic and social repair, Morrison's literary work is exemplary. As her Nobel Prize adjudicators acknowledge: "She delves into the language itself, a language she wants to liberate from the fetters of race. And she addresses us with the luster of poetry" (Grimes 1993, 2). Morrison's novels school us in a poetic language that teeters on the knife edge of the racist construction of human. Her use of affected language repairs humanity from the ruins of dehumanizing violence, armed with a damning ontology of being that positions some as human and some as "Other." Morrison's literary feat attempts the seemingly impossible: she reclaims a bent and broken humanity from the silenced annals of terrible traumatic history.

Beloved begins eighteen years after Sethe and her daughter Denver have escaped from institutional slavery and the horrific events that took place at the Sweet Home Plantation. The plot pivots on the infanticide of Beloved at her mother's hand; an act that Sethe interprets as a mother's revolt from the institution of human degradation to which she and her children are hopelessly bound. According to Edgerton, the infanticide is taken by Morrison from the archives of slave narratives and reworked in this fictional account: "The seed for Morrison's *Beloved* is the story of Margaret Garner[3] who killed her daughter and attempted to kill her other children and herself rather than return or turn them over to slavery" (Edgerton 1995, 344). The slave-testimony of Garner is many times retold. Still, as Edgerton notes, "these stories did not honor an interior life for either Margaret Garner or, of course, for her baby, nor for those the baby represented" (ibid., 345). *Beloved* is Morrison's attempt to honor Garner, the baby and "the sixty million and more" by writing into fiction and historical memory the devastated *interior* lives of those enslaved by dehumanizing narratives of existence (Morrison 2004, epigraph).

With a plot line that inserts itself into the ruined interior world of Sethe, Morrison implies that translating the ex-slave's shattered internal world is critical to rewriting African American and colonial history and our humanity. For Morrison, it is not enough for societies to try to make historical amends for crimes of humanity solely through the political avenues and public discourses of health, education, and the law: the interior worlds of affected communities injured by social ruin also require redress. If social reparation offers an apology or restitution for social and material crimes committed against humanity, often left unaddressed are internal social injuries reeling within individuals and spanning generations. In this regard, rebuilding ruined inside lives is as complex as rebuilding villages (Mishra Tarc 2011).

Morrison's novel acknowledges the role of the inner and emotional world in symbolizing a meaningful life for self and others. As we saw in the case of Elizabeth Costello, reading depends on already internalized symbolic formations. Previous experiences with literacy and in life give new shape and form to the language we use to interpret the self in relation to others. The denial of inner and emotional worlds in literacy robs children of recourse to their internal and interpretive resources and experiences of existence. Instrumental forms of literacy can form for the child an instrumental sense of herself void of emotional content that gives one the fundamental basis for attaching to people and things. But more than this: Oliver (2002) insists that reducing people's lives to materiality denies them their inner life and access to the significance of their humanity. Perhaps this is why material forms of reparation, though necessary, rarely support individuals to live again well in communities reeling from mass violence. To live well and survive, one needs loving forms of symbolic representation and a healing language with which to bring significance to one's humanity.

Inscribing the "Other" non- or subhuman, the oppressor deems her as without the "human" capabilities to dream, to have faith, to think, to be. When one's existence is collapsed with material realities, the "Other" is subject to preformed and objective representations rather than afforded with a unique and loving means with which to represent herself (Fanon 1967; Spivak 1999). Following Fanon (1967), Oliver argues:

> The internalization process of oppression and colonization results in the collapse of internal space,—the psyche, mind, or soul. In order to render the oppressed inhuman, the oppressors represent them as animals at the mercy of their bodily instincts with no access to an interior mental life. (2001, 24)

Dehumanizing representations of oneself are not only internally inscribed through forms of knowledge. More insinuating are internalizing forms of literacy that give rise to discourses of social hate and violence. For example, if children are given dehumanizing language by their mothers with which to communicate themselves, this language is not only at work in their talk; more damning perhaps is the child's internalization of a repertoire of words imbued with diminished meaning that limits her capacity to think apart from those egregious representations. And yet, remarkably, a child recognizes the injury in statements used to demean her existence; she can, incredibly, summon up internal defenses to creatively wage word war with the injustice some words inflict. Literacy gives us the recourse to stage revolt and renewal with forms of language. Literacy can make us suffer and regress; it also can help us to repair and grow.

In her novels and essays, Morrison indicts the more damning of children's language experiences in processes of literacy they learn in school. In school the child learns the legitimate proper names that render a unique idea and existence of oneself, "Other."

> It is a question of education, because racism is a scholarly pursuit. It's all over the world, I am convinced. But that's not the way people were born to live. I'm talking about racism that is taught, institutionalized. Everybody remembers the first time they were taught that part of the human race was Other. That's a trauma. It's as though I told you that your left hand is not part of your body. (in Angelo and Morrison 1989, 25)

Confronting literacies of dehumanization in her novel inventions of human existence, Morrison takes seriously the work of language in othering a life. In *Beloved,* she shows that a dehumanizing literacy begins when Schoolteacher uses the name *slave* to position blacks beneath a superior Self defined as White,[4] Male, and Human. As portrayed in the novel, the event of literacy is one where the child is rendered less than human in a word: *animal, nigger, slave, dumb.* The proper name "Slave" makes certain claim to the other's body and justifies, for Schoolteacher, unthinkable acts of dehumanization of blacks.

The chilling events that take place in the "fictional" school are eerily and orderly depicted as one might expect of any schoolhouse scene. In this "school of thought," distorted normative discourse is taken to its extreme, producing "monstrous lessons" for and about the other (Willinsky 1998). Morrison depicts instrumental literacy pedagogy as enacting the most violating aspects of Western symbolic logic. "Schoolteacher" overdetermines a number of conventional and progressive pedagogical practices to ensure that his students are led to prejudicial conclusions about the slaves. His favorite lessons take up his theory of the "animal characteristics" of blacks. This dehumanizing theory explicitly denies blacks the possibility of an interior life where resides the creative capacity to dream, think, and symbolically renew. The pupils learn to "read and write" the slaves according to their so-called animal-traits. In one lesson they are asked to list, catalogue, and compare Sethe's "human" and "animal" characteristics. When the pupils grow uncomfortable with the task, Schoolteacher punishes them for showing a sliver of concern for the bodies they examine: "No, no. That's not the way. I told you to put her human characteristics on the left; her animal ones on the right. And don't forget to *line them up*" (Morrison 2004, 228; italics added). The pupils are taught to conduct "scientific experiments" on Sethe to verify Schoolteacher's racist ideas of her. These experiments are externally conducted in utter disregard for Sethe. The students learn about the dehumanized other through the logic and justification of racism in the familiar forms of a Schoolteacher's knowledge: pronouncements, lists, discriminations, explanations, and unrelenting discipline. And when one slave, Sixo, contests Schoolteacher's knowledge, the rules of the discourse change. Language is twisted and turned to support Schoolteacher's demeaning pedagogy because the "definitions belong to the definers—not the defined" (ibid., 225). For his verbal revolt, Sixo is severely punished.

Imaging the extreme inner effects of Schoolteacher's pedagogy of literacy in the lives of student and slaves, Morrison brings to fiction the position I advance in this book: how the child enters into and is taught to use language is critical to her subject formation. In his discussion of South African apartheid, Derrida (1986) cogently argues this point. In school and other social institutions, literacy in racist constructions of the human find its way into the minds and bodies of Blacks, Coloureds, and Whites. Racism has to have a word, writes Derrida, and this word, *race,* institutes a dehumanizing logic that partitions off one's humanity from the rest of human existence. He specifically indicts the judicial and education systems instituting racist language as the means and ends by which racist violence is imagined and enacted (Derrida 1986, 331).

> There's no racism without a language. The point is not that acts of racial violence are only words but rather that they have to have a word. Even though it offers the excuse of blood, colour, birth—or, rather, *because* it uses this naturalist and sometimes creationist discourse—racism always betrays the perversion of a man, the "talking animal." It institutes, declares, writes, inscribes, prescribes. A system of marks, it outlines space in order to assign forced residence or to close off borders. It does not discern, it discriminates. (ibid.)

Derrida suggests the existence of a baby born to a system of Apartheid and/or extreme racism is sequestered off from humanity by the inscription of racial traits even before she can speak of herself through the language of the other. This radical severance of her existence from humanity has devastating consequences for individuals and communities. If the oppressed are severely affected by the oppressor's severance of their humanity from their self, the oppressor is mentally afflicted with a diminished capacity to see the other's humanity as critical to his own (Freire 1982). Insidious are violent and differently manifesting effects of racist severing of the insides of blacks and whites from their humanity. This severance of inner existence from social life finds its extreme parallel in the unthinkable institutions we build to sequester, enslave, and violate the sanctity of human life.

As with Beloved, the child is born into a language of race, into a discursive world with a deformed idea of the baby. Her human status or nonstatus is consolidated in the mere event of birth of a person carrying certain traits. People suggest that children are not inherently racist, however often is the proper names given to children to identify, classify, and form ideas of themselves and others. As Derrida (1986) stresses, race does not simply discern, it discriminates, rendering to some bodies a human worth less than others. Because we all need the other's language to communicate, the child born in a racist state has little choice but to use, to her own and the other's detriment, a discriminating language to narrate her existence against those of others. There seems to be no way out of the narrative binds of "normative" existence that we are tied to by literacy at birth.

In the novel, Sethe decides that there is no way out of the narrative of slavery and the discursive shackles holding captive her thought and mind. The grim realization of her child born into a language of social hatred that renders her at birth black, slave, "Other" leaves Sethe utterly helpless to save her baby from insertion into that history. This terrible knowledge of her baby's prefabricated nonhuman existence drives Sethe to commit a finite act. She severs the baby's existence from the world of shackles in which Beloved is born. And with this act Sethe does the unthinkable: she commits the baby to death by her mother's hand.

The infanticide has garnered much critical attention despite the imaginative freedoms afforded to us by fiction. Even the idea of such a childless future fills critics and readers with dread. However, when read psychoanalytically, with a Freudian story of infants and mothers that features a psychical murder, the murder of the baby at her mother's hand takes on new psychological significance. I read the infancy as Morrison's imaginative bid to repair the interior lives of the slaves through psychical reparation afforded to them by a terrible return to the potential and promise of black baby's infancy, cut off before she can exist, in the racist state of slavery.

Although intellectually and morally challenging, the fictional infanticide of Beloved serves a psychical end. In Freud's plot line, murder between mother and child is a psychical event. Navigating her personhood apart from the mother, the baby psychically murders the mother to give birth to her self. Matricide, as Kristeva suggests, "is a biological and psychic necessity, the sine qua non condition of our individuation" (1992, 27–28). To become someone apart from the mother, we commit murder to her in our minds.

In *Beloved*, Morrison stages the reverse; the mother kills the baby, which allows for the narration of Sethe's second psychical rebirth through Beloved's ghostly return. Character and the reader are deeply affected by the dead baby's return as they plunge in and out of the events of Beloved's infanticide. The revisiting of the scene of the crime winds through reality and fiction, history and memory, conscious and unconscious event.

Psychically renewing thought, language, and the idea of human, Morrison returns the reader to the internal life of infancy and the infant. However, the conceptually extreme means of this return to infancy is unthinkable, even in fiction. Although I am posing the infanticide as a psychical fiction, the novel implicates the "real" status of the baby. Infancy, as generator and end of the future of humankind, hangs tenuously in the balance.

Our real-life thoughts and experiences and those of the fictional characters psychologically make the infant's murder difficult to bear. Even if we remind ourselves that this is fiction, we can still be disturbed, as we saw with Costello, by the felt as a real experience that an imagined world presents. The novel is also affected by the fictional infanticide event, and heavily grapples with the implications of Sethe's crime against the baby as the means and ends by which she might eliminate her child's participation in a racist system of being. Both character and reader are deeply troubled by Sethe's decision to kill her baby to save Beloved from the proper name, Slave. Moral repercussions of Sethe's unthinkable act wind through the novel, the reader's mind, and the novel's characters. This moral aporia is taken up most memorably in the voice of Paul D.

> "What you did was wrong, Sethe."
>
> "I should have gone on back there? Taken my babies back there?"
>
> "There could have been a way. Some other way."
>
> "What way?"
>
> "You got two feet, Sethe, not four," he said, and right then a forest sprang up between them; trackless and quiet. (Morison 2004, 194)

Despite Paul D's gentle rebuke and plea to refind her humanity, Sethe refuses to accept for her children the dehumanized versions of existence offered to them by Schoolteacher. The question of right and wrong is too raw for her to contemplate at the other's insistence. This impasse is lodged at the novel's kernel and the reader's difficult experience of reading.

Morrison does not leave the question of what happened to the baby to the moral judgment of the narrator, Sethe, Paul D., or the reader. The ghost leaves the matter of the existential and moral meanings of the infanticide unsettled. Morrison seems to imply that extreme measures are needed to address racist violence of the past haunting the present. And yet, in Beloved's vengeful return Morrison indicates that these measures must be taken without knowing in advance, yet with painstaking regard for what is best for the baby. The nonverbal baby has a say in the future of her existence in a racist world. The adult cannot singlehandedly decide what is best for the baby's future even in a cruel world. With the baby's angry, egregious return, Morrison demonstrates that psychologically and actually severing the baby from the symbolic order producing the ruined world is unsustainable for Sethe and her children and us all.

Some feminist critics metaphorically interpret the infanticide as a triumph of the maternal symbolic over the racist, patriarchal symbolic order (Wyatt 1993). However, this interpretation seems to miss Morrison's point. She seems to insist in this difficult reckoning with the traumatic memory of Beloved that victory of one human over the other comes at a terrible price. The unbearable, interminable suffering wrought by Sethe's infanticide is felt by all, indicating that no one, no *one,* can simply destroy or abandon the symbolic order or the other or the social world, by which they are given existence.[5] As Sethe painfully attempts to confront her part in a violating and violent past, she is confronted with her desperate need of language and others to make amends to herself, the infant, and the world. A broken-down language supports Sethe to dig deep inside for a literacy that repairs the excesses of symbolic and actual violence enacted on her mind and body and supports her to somehow find the internal impetus, to begin to live again and with others.

In school and at home, Morrison highlights the importance of hanging on to language and the world it produces despite its harm. A scene in the novel finds Baby Suggs, Sethe's mother-in-law, driven to abandon the Word[6] after the "blood spill in her backyard" and "after sixty years of losing children to the people who chewed up her life and spit it out like a fishbone" (Morrison 2004, 208–209). When Baby Suggs, a preacher, gifted with the Word, falls mute at her own bidding, another slave, Stamp Paid, fights hard to convince her otherwise. For

Stamp Paid, the Word is her gift to speak the Truth of the slave's right to human existence.

> "Listen here girl," he told her, "you can't quit the Word. It's given to you to speak. You can't quit the Word, I don't care what all happen to you." (ibid., 209)

Morrison cannot end the story of literacy in a racist school of thought. Nor can she end the story with the infant's severance from a racist history. Nor can she end the story with the end of literacy. But as she indicates in the pageless, last pages of the novel: "It was not a story to pass on"; a human story void of infancy, of language, of other is not one that offers a viable end.

Positioned in this aporia, Morrison's word work embarks upon an experimental, *internal* renewal of the infant's language occasioned by a psychical infanticide. Generated from this hard mental space is a story of symbolic repair written in the stuff of dreams. Her poetic depiction of infancy's return to the dead slave's dead inner world stunningly renarrates a story of cut-off human potential located in internal life. Her novel restoration of the slave's interior world testifies to the creative possibility of freedom of mind and thought afforded by literary art. And with an infantile renewal, Morrison implies that resignifying forms of language can lessen the violence of dehumanizing discourses of the human: an other-oriented literacy can also address dehumanizing forms of language with real material effects. Scrutinizing and adapting our use and pedagogy of language might free the child's existence to the world's offerings rather than keep her mind and body enslaved to proper names designating a species, a normative body, a gender, a race, a culture, and religion. Acknowledging that the child is given to herself when she is given to words that give her the world, we might take more care with the words we use to introduce her precious existence in a continually renewing world (Arendt 2006). We might also support the symbolic capacities of young children to learn to represent themselves and others void of binary or reductive logic tethering their unique bodies to existing hierarchical representations of human beings. To develop a literacy that acknowledges its difficult beginnings, as I have been insisting throughout the trajectory of this book, we might follow Morrison's lead and return our literate practice of language to the dream-words of infancy.

Rebirthing Language: A Baby's Venom

> Who would have thought that a little old baby could harbor so much rage?
>
> —*Beloved*

Beloved returns reading to infancy. But Beloved is no ordinary infant. Part ghost, part interiority, and part human, Beloved comes back to life to reclaim language and existence from mother. And this is no ordinary mother. The mother's capacity for communication is severely muted. She is near catatonic, subject to umimaginable depression. Stuck in the house with her daughter, Sethe is all but left for dead.

If not for the infant's unwelcome second coming, Sethe might have indefinitely succumbed to sorrow. Beloved jolts Sethe unceremoniously out of her dead state. Enlivened by her baby's rebirth Sethe is forced to respond. However, caring for a psychotic ghost baby is no easy task. Cut short of life, the infant is teeming with rage. The infant's murderous affects, aimed at the mother, overwhelm. These affects are placed between words to wreak havoc, fragment by fragment, phrase by phrase, word by word, on our reading of Sethe's forced infantile summons back to the symbolic, social world.

Morrison figures the time and effect of infancy on the human psyche in the ghost of Beloved. And if extreme are the conditions giving way to the infant's rebirth, this baby's phantastic situation resembles the furious, inconsolable, and insatiable one described by Klein. According to Klein, in infancy the baby is plagued with sadistic feelings toward his parents and first objects: "[T]he child's sadistic attacks have for their object both father and mother, who are in phantasy bitten, torn, cut or stamped to bits" (1930, 219). At the height of sadism and in re-infancy, Beloved is psychotic with persecutory anxiety and enraged at the slightest provocation, biting and clawing her way into recognizable existence.

Beloved's ghostly and unexpected arrival is as overwhelming as that of a real infant. Upon Beloved's return the infant begins to take over every aspect of the mother's existence. Living in House 124 is unbearable. Sethe and Denver are subject to persecutory voices and to the slamming and knocking of "spite" ("of a baby's venom") (Morrison 2004, 3). The suffocating presence in the house suspends them in deferred time and space. Each attempt to excise the presence of

Beloved fails. The baby's need is everywhere, sucking the life out of everyone it meets.

In adult-form and with adult language, Beloved expresses the somatic qualities of Klein's infant. Emerging from "water," and not knowing from where she comes, Beloved is inexplicably driven toward the breast/mother. The infant emerges from the water with "lungs that hurt." She seems drunk and unable to properly coordinate her arms and legs (2004, 60). Insatiable with thirst, cold and drowsy, Beloved is unable to control her bladder and bowels. Her sounds are emitted in murmurs and breathing. Upon viewing her face Sethe's bladder fills up and she becomes incontinent with amniotic fluid: "There was no stopping water breaking from a breaking womb" (ibid., 61).

Images of pregnancy and childbirth alongside unthinkable violence saturate the retelling of Sethe's traumatic memory. These images also flash back to the horrific birth of blacks into the institution of slavery. In fragmented images of rebirth return the scenes of severance of the sacred domain and practice of motherhood at the slaveholder's vicious hand.

Lorraine Liscio suggests that Morrison fashions the prelinguistic code of infancy into poetic discourse to "[resist] the deadly conventions of white narrative."

> Morrison's narrator privileges a perception and prelinguistic code of communication associated with infancy. Such communication offers an alternate mode meant like other rhetorical figuration used by black writers to break white hegemony's control and create their own identity through naming themselves (Elison's Invisible Man is another obvious example). . . . In *Beloved*, the agent unseating the father's law, white language, is above all the black mother-infant daughter bond, a doubly invisible participant in white patriarchal history. (Liscio 1992, 39)

In Morrison's narrative the prelinguistic inner life code of the dead baby is designed to combat the violence of symbolic law. The code tears apart the narrative with the force of its affects. However, because the code is infused with traumatic infantile affects, it is radically *unlike* the rhetorical or ideological figurations used by other black writers to revolt against black enslavement. Morrison uses dreamwords to invoke the felt presence of traumatized infantile affects and overwhelm the authority of symbolic law. "Traumatic language," Juliet Mitchell writes, "is a verbal version of the visual language of dreams; words are metaphors, similes, and symbolic equations; they have the status of inner but not internal objects; they become expressions of feeling rather than of meaning" (1998, 132). Accordingly, the prelinguistic code in the novel visualizing the dead baby is starkly literal. Words take the place of loss rather than articulate loss. Words stand in for loss rather than provide easy access to the meanings of loss. Feeling poses a challenge to words as words testify to the ghost baby's felt traumatic presence.

To be rudely placed in the oppressive environment of interiority, and made to read the horrific events through Sethe's ruined mental state, is demanding on the reader. Morrison abruptly returns us to the infantile source of language's wound, the severed traumatic affect, and the novel can be difficult to follow. The human story Morrison excavates is told in the language of suffering. She also resituates a "language there all along,"[7] in the processes of healing (74). The refound, stored maternal language is not one of hope or despair. Rather, this language is structured in and as the hallucinating dream state of the infant where one's felt existence is perpetually shaking. With the novel regression into infantile mental processes, Sethe, and the reader, begin to make sense of the present angrily haunted by the past.

The Reparative Potential of Literacy

Words can hurt. They can also heal and renew. Klein's (1937) theory of reparation takes its basis in symbolization, a process of excavating stored and found internal language that supports the child to respond to her feelings of loss of mother. Psychoanalysis theorizes a double function of symbolization where one's internal resources for communication are built up through the exchange of maternally given and offered words. Literacy can support a more gentle entry into the external world and to the adult's demand that children "communicate." Carefully choosing and substituting nurturing words to approximate the baby's hard feelings, the mother begins to account for the baby's lost and found sense of reality. In this accounting of her existence the baby receives her "first impressions of love" tentatively offered in the mother's words (Britzman 2009b). Literacy, in this view, need not be held to representation but instead, to what Andre Green describes as the psychical dynamics of loss and love narrating a symbol (2008, 80).

Morrison positions the slaves' efforts to symbolize a traumatic past as critical to their development of a literacy bearing witness to their existence. Without the terrifying return of the baby, Sethe and Denver might be forever enslaved to deadening traumatic affect. Affects wage inside and across the character's lives in their desperate attempts to find words that might reckon with a lost world and existence in the aftermath of atrocity. Together, characters grieve their loss to self and community at the hand of a merciless society through the work of symbolization and internal repair, through the work of mourning.

The House at 124 is one of weird mourning. Inserted into this creepy place, the reader, along with Sethe and Denver, is cut off from the world and subject to the cries and creaks of the baby's memory. In *Melancholia and Mourning*, Freud characterizes normal mourning as a withdrawal of the self from the world. Impaired is the mourner's capacity to adopt a new interest. She refuses to engage in activities outside the internal context of the loss of the other (Freud 1917, 243). The mourner's temporary retreat from external reality is necessary for her to engage in the work of symbolizing a profound loss. Working through the loss involves "bringing up" and "hypercathecting" memories of the lost object bit by bit. Mourning also invokes the mourner's feelings of anger, blame, and reproach directed toward the dead. These felt memories of the other contained in profound loss compromise the mourner's wish to remain locked in the memory of the other: the other's memory also recalls the harsh reality of the external world. Slowly and in time and with the aid of memory, in lieu and recall of external reality, the mourner loosens her hold on the beloved person's loss.

When we open the book and the door to House 124, we find a mother and her daughter, overcome by the loss of the infant Beloved: grief has turned inside into them both. Morrison depicts Sethe and Denver caught in the death grip of the baby's ghost and unable to resume healthy functioning. Freud deemed this extreme incapacity to let go and be let go of by loss as melancholia, a version of mourning gone awry. While aspects of both processes insinuate themselves in each other, the main and difficult obstacle of melancholia is the mourner's inability to separate the self from the loss of the other. In extreme cases, as is with Sethe, the self experiences the loss of the other as death to the self. Sethe's "dead" sense of herself is tied up in the dead baby Beloved. Melancholia literally takes shape in Sethe's dead state, unable to rouse herself and take leave of a house haunted by a baby ghost.

In mourning, the egoistic distance between the self and other allows the mourner to direct her feelings of anger and grief toward the object. In melancholia, the ego narcissistically appropriates the memory of the other. Feelings of self-reproach, revulsion, and blame ordinarily directed at the loss are directed at one's own ego. In her inability to separate loss of the other from loss of the self and, by extension the world, the melancholic displays "extraordinary diminution in his self regard, an impoverishment of his ego on a grand scale" (Freud 1917, 246).

In Beloved's return to the melancholic scene of the mother's terrible crime, Morrison imagines a "social" version of a psychical event of mourning gone wrong. Deadened from relentlessly beating up on her self, Sethe is unable to rouse out of an ego unbelievably devastated by the loss of Beloved. Loss of the baby turns on her, splits her open, turns into herself, and breaks down Sethe. The return of the ghost baby, in the haunted memory of Beloved, is not as a new arrival but as a new edition of the unspeakable trauma of her death by Sethe's hand. Beloved's reappearance to the melancholic scene is the means by which Sethe can rebirth herself from the ravages of incredible grief. The return of the infant, a return Morrison stages in Sethe's dead inner life, plunges Sethe into the world and animates Sethe's internal resources to find, recover, and rebuild the ruins of her devastated ego.

The summons of the ghost to the melancholic scene electrifies Sethe out of a catatonic state into one that might begin to mourn the baby, even while the mother can barely tolerate to contemplate meanings of the past. The ghost baby enlivens the dead mother's internal world, locating her ruined capacity to respond. Her refound maternal compulsion to respond to the baby shakes Sethe out of a devastated existence.

Curiously, we find and rebuild the resources of a ruined internal world in our painful yet necessary deliberation of loss. Grief does not operate as deliberation at the level of judgment; instead, in our unexpected regression to infancy we are given the chance to tap into grief-stricken internal resources that once supported and oriented us to live. Morrison literally figures this necessary infantile return in the figure of Beloved and in the work of mourning, embodied by one's affected reading experience. Reader and Sethe wade through a narrative teeming with affects, fragmented realities, and competing symbols. The charged literary experience of psychical and emotional labor is critical to Sethe's and the reader's capacity to articulate the social meanings of Beloved.

To make meaning of traumatic history, we must first mourn the unthinkable event of the infant's terminated existence subject to a cruel and merciless social world. The work of mourning for Sethe is as extreme as the trauma that haunts. As she bravely and painstakingly contemplates the meanings of Beloved's traumatic loss through memory, she refinds her internal capacity to speak, restore, and repair the inner world. The work of mourning follows the treacherous movement of grief as it travels from the remote and mute internal state of the mourner to the surface of the symbolic, all the while gasping for words that give meaning to irreparable existence. Reading as a work of mourning also supports an opening for the reader. Tapping into our sympathetic, shaken insides, the novel supports the reader's interpretive capacity to foster a new regard for the other's traumatic history, which denigrates and diminishes the whole of humanity.

The shattered language in which trauma is narrated provides the basis of Sethe's internal repair. It is critical that a (m)other bears witness to Sethe's barely communicable testimony of extreme suffering. Paul D., the witness, is necessary for her to find words. The two embark upon a worded process of exchanging memories where the missing pieces of one's own memory are filled in with memories of the other. Testing reality by crosschecking and accounting for symbolized memories, the two begin to restore to their lives renewed meanings of existence they had actively suppressed.

Symbolization of their traumatic history proves excruciating. The ex-slaves' attempts to remember are further obstructed by their struggle to find words to put torn-apart memories together. Morrison depicts the former slaves' traumatic relationship to language as the infant's—ambivalent and anxious. Each is suspicious of words even as each depends on them to make meaning. Language has, after all, harmed the slaves unforgivably. Schoolteacher inscribes Sethe's body with animal imagery. Paul D. is silenced with the mule bit. Sixo stops speaking English after refusing to speak the debased language of the slaveholders. These injuries, in turn, cause each to temporarily or permanently stop speaking.

Try as they might, the characters of Beloved cannot quit the Word. Morrison's word-work demonstrates that what is needed in the slave community is a renewed relation to symbols and the symbolic order in the aftermath of trauma. Renewed symbols brought forward by the feeling force of poetry become their lifeline, their symbolic way to communicate incomprehensible experiences. Klein writes, "[Symbolism] is the basis of the subject's relation to the outside world and to reality in general" (1930, 221). Sharing her terrible experiences with an other who hears and re-sounds her words to her is critical to stabilizing Seth's inner self. The aggressive encounter with Beloved sets the conditions for Sethe's psychic repair. Co-constructing symbols to speak of self-suffering rebuilds the psyche and restores the internal world.

Morrison stages the infantile work of mourning in the formal structure of the plot. Narrative is fragmented. Meaning is deferred. Grief and rage are everywhere. At the height of mourning, narrative breaks down and meaning regresses into poetic discourse.

Mourning is also figured in the fraught relation between the dead baby and melancholic mother. The ghost baby overwhelms. She agitates all around her. Her haunting demands leave Sethe spent. Beloved's relentless presence drives a wedge between Sethe and her daughter and Paul D. Beloved drives Sethe to the point of mental and physical exhaustion, to the point where she can no longer tolerate the memory of Beloved. The ghostly demands on her mental and physical state are too much. "Diminished and shamed" by the infant, Sethe finally lets the baby leave her self (Morrison 2004, 295).

Letting go of Beloved's ghost provides Sethe with the impetus for mourning, for internal recovery. The novel signals its traumatic release of the dead baby's ghost in a splitting narrative refashioned into "the visual language of dreams" (Mitchell 1988, 132).

> When I put that headstone up I wanted to lay in there with you, put your head on my shoulder and keep you warm, and I would have if Bulgar and Howard and Denver didn't need me, because my mind was homeless then. I couldn't lay down with you then. No matter how much I wanted to. I couldn't lay down nowhere in peace, back then. Now I can. I can sleep like the drowned, have mercy. She come back to me, my daughter, and she is mine. (Morrison 2004, 241)

Letting go of the ghost baby, Sethe is restored from the melancholic dead. Her first attempts to articulate the meanings of and take responsibility for the dead baby are both structured by and radically outside of the existing symbolic order. The formal construction of the monologues is also very unlike the rest of the novel. This flowing poetic prose provides the reader with some release from the bombardment of affects characterizing Beloved's return. With Sethe, we feel rid of the ghost baby, and hopefully for good. And yet we cannot quite let go of the memory of the dead baby. Her unforgettable encounter leaves us "marked" long after the novel ends.

Reparation is the name Klein gives to the baby's symbolizing a new regard for self and other from the ravages of internal suffering and grief. Psychical reparation allows one to make social amends with oneself and other. In infancy we are constantly given to grief and reparation because we are losing our mother all the time. Mourning a perpetual loss of our mother, we use words to make her return. And in these words filled with mother we are given many meanings that support us to have new regard for mother. The significance held in words that heal comes to symbolize our lifelong and continually altering relation to and from mother. The significance contained in healing words of mother are held poignantly in mind. Dehumanizing violence broke down Sethe but physical acts of degradation did not completely destroy the significance of her existence. We can survive a merciless social reality with our capacity to repair the real and imagined hateful damage others do to ourselves with our mother's loving significant resources, which we carry inside.

Through mourning, we come to terms with the social fact that, for better and worse, we have no choice but to let go of our (m)other. This process is reversed in the novel where the baby's ghost returns to the mother. With Beloved's return the mother is given a second chance, through the adult baby's affects, to find significance and restore her broken insides. In Sethe's actual and internal fall to infancy, figured by Beloved, she is given the internal resources to live again, and this time with renewed and faltering communicable significance.

> The pain experienced in the slow process of testing reality in the work of mourning thus seems to be partly due to the necessity, not only to renew the links to the external world and thus continuously to re-experience the loss, but at the same time and by means of this to rebuild with anguish the inner world, which is felt to be in danger of deteriorating and collapsing. (Klein 1940, 354)

Klein insists that this infantile process so necessary to the baby's subject formation is recalled each time we experience loss, both ordinary and extreme in a lifetime of coexistence. Morrison depicts psychical reparation through mourning as reflexive internal rebuilding of the anguish of the inner world socially injured by atrocity and mass violence. Drawing forth and speaking of memories in a poetic language of infancy refuels Sethe's prior incapacity to reestablish her links to her loved ones in the external world. She refinds a memoried language of the mother that was "there all along." Memory arrives slowly, broken in fragments. Trauma returns to her in dreams. As she begins to communicate words metabolized with infancy, symbols feel less labored and resigned with new meaning.

For Klein, the capacity to repair one's self through the symbolization of loss humanizes us; loss gives us insight into the feelings of vulnerability and dependence that found our humanity. Above all, Klein viewed reparation as critical to the development of healthy human relations. Literacy begets reparation as it is through symbolizing minor losses to the self at the hands of our mother that we find the language to continually rebirth ourselves and our relation to the world. Through a literacy of the Other we relearn a language, which reckons with the implication of others haunting our existence. Ultimately, *Beloved* offers readers a dreamwork language of "mental expression" by which to heal ourselves and to consider the articulations of an existence that is difficult to conceive.

In the wake of Toni Morrison's *Beloved*, we might reorient literacy as a practice that renews, from the ravages of social ruin, human relations. Language supports us to excavate intra- and interhuman histories that inform all our relations. Literacy as a form of reparation for the more unthinkable of human situations can create a renewed story of other forms of human existence.

After wreaking her infantile rage on everyone with whom she comes into contact, Beloved departs as inexplicably as she arrived. Sethe has no choice but to return to actual others in the world. Letting go of Beloved, Sethe moves outside of herself and toward others: "Sethe is running away from her, running, and she feels the emptiness in the hand Sethe has been holding. Now she is running into the faces of the people out there, joining them and leaving Beloved behind. Alone. Again" (Morrison 2004, 309). Still, if she is released from the death grip of trauma she is not released, as her grief indicates, from the memory of her baby.

"She was my best thing." . . .

[Paul D.] "You your best thing, Sethe. You are." . . .

"Me, me?" (2004, 321–22)

Remaining, after *Beloved*, is the question of where one's human subjectivity resides. The force of these fragments suggests that, for the slave, the mother, the baby, the writer, the reader, and the world, what deserves the name *humanity* is still under revision, still yet to be. The breaking-down Sethe reminds us that our need of the other's words, psychically and socially, for better and for worse, constitutes the fragility and resilience of our prone-to-breakdown selves, our humanity. Renewing the meanings of herself through a plunge back into infancy, Sethe finds the internal resources to live and to live better with others. Loss, both ordinary and extreme, animates the internal means to find and remake anew a self broken by social violence and ruin. Our feelings of loss are not produced from the same social content or context as Sethe's but we can be affected nonetheless by a fictional character's return to life from the deadly depths of unfathomable loss. And through our reading, we too can be renewed by a plunge back into infancy and an unthinkable history that we also thought we forgot.

Through language that rips to the core of terrible human history, Morrison's novel teaches us that life killing is the racist order of being offered to children in school. This story of a human existence cut off from potential and teeming life "cannot be passed on." The lack of meaning that demeaning language can have for students, even for those whose identities we might presume are supported by the dominant order, can and often do lead to unthinkable consequences. Social exclusion is not simply a denial of economic opportunities but also a denial of the symbolic means by which meaning can be made of one's life and the lives of others. Existential significance is vital to one's learning to be and to be in good relation with others in the world. Denying the child's struggle for meaning in her lifelong relation to language also denies her precious access to the complexities of unrepresentable experience that structure human existence. The child learns that language is the representative of her humanity in stories that support her to "know oneself" and others. If we disregard the connection between literacy and ontic mythologies, we unwittingly commit the tiny new arrivals to distorting narratives of social life and cruelly prefabricate a unique potential for existence. We can reconceptualize literacy as learning to "read" the vast systems of psychical and social meaning circulating in the words we use to story our humanity—a humanity that depends on the combined effort of the parent-schoolteacher's nurturing pedagogical support of the child's entry into the symbolic and the social. A literacy informed by (our) unthinkable infancy learns to both bear and infuse language with the generative and destructive life-giving "thing" that holds the meaning of all of our existence.

6

Before and After Words

Hold fast to the word, then reach for the experience behind it.

—J. M. Coetzee, "The Problem of Evil"

From the moment we are born until the day we die, we live with language. And language lives with us. As we enter into language it begins to play with us, and we play back. Language secures our fleeting selves to a time and space, to a name and identity, to a family and nation. At times, we are caught up in the rapture of the tongue—words speak to us, reach to the core of our being, our belonging. Words help. Other times, language threatens. Words are forced. Our words are not our own. We cannot speak our minds. We stop speaking. Words hurt.

As a kindergarten teacher, I watched helplessly as children struggled to articulate their desires through words that often frustrated their impassioned efforts to convey to me a sense of their being. Emotional outbursts inevitably ensued as children became overwhelmed and enthralled by the educational imperative to "narrate thyself" with a limited yet strangely workable vocabulary. As teachers, we can view children's struggles to say something as a disturbance, a provocation, or as a behavioral challenge when more often than not they are trying to convey an inner significance lost on words. Sometimes the words available to children fail to do justice to the emotional activity circulating within their sentient bodies. Other times, with great joy and exuberance a word feels just right and a linguistic accomplishment gives voice to an expression of profound meaning.

We have not been schooled to think of language as something that we inhabit and live. Conventional literacy teaches us to think of words as outside of our bodies. We isolate words to learn them. We think words in our minds. We disassociate words from experience. We are taught that words can replace us and our innermost thoughts and feelings. "Use your words," we tell our children when they are at a loss. "That's not the right word," we tell students when they stumble to describe their situation. "Say what you mean," we demand of others, as if it is only a question of precision, as if words are a given and not also received.

We are taught to think of language as the neutral and objective medium by which to represent the world. We use words to stake masterful claim to the truth. But language is beyond full mastery. Language can take hold of us rather than be held to a word. The other's language shelters our strange feelings and thoughts. The other's words leave us open to question, to exposing our inside, to making new thoughts of our self.

We are subject to the other's language, through which we learn to word an existence and sense of self. Our subjectivity to a life of language is both hospitable and alienating. We need the other's language to be someone in a time and place not of our making. The other's language gives us a self as it voids us of self.

For better and worse, language indelibly affects us. Our parents gift us with magical words at infancy. In childhood, these words gain public and social significance and lose their magic. In school, we learn to line up, order, and name ourselves against the bodies of others. We use words to hurt those whom we deem smaller, weaker, weirder, and dumber than us. We use words to defend our friends from the violence contained in those words. We use words as if our lives depended on it.

These school days lessons direct our lives through a lifetime of thought. As presumably self-loving, free-thinking and acting beings, it can be hard to see our lives led by the other's words. We too easily forget to acknowledge that the other's words move us when we singlehandedly move mountains.

This book uses literature to construct an other-oriented theory of literacy. And yet, it was a hurt child in my classroom and not a novel that first alerted me, conceptually, to the co-constructed situation of literacy. Observing him virtually exploding with affects of rage and pleasure when attempting to put his thoughts into words, I began to rely on my training in English language literature to read a child's fabulous symbolic constructions. These constructions storied the child's life in ways that both supported and alienated him from himself and others. I found a fictive quality in the formation of the child's words and sentences, an aesthetic quality I broadly term "emotional." I did not subject the emotional expression of his inner world to a single literary framework; I instead relied on my trained and unorthodox reading of the unreliable emotional content contained in novels. I read this child's insides the way I read novels. Together we made literary interpretations of an inside world thrown into chaos as an effect of personal and social trauma. The method of reading on which I relied was speculative, perhaps resembling an analysis or deconstruction or both; I found evidence for my interpretation in emotional clues piecing together the fragmented structure of a child's communication. I struggled to bracket my personal histories and feelings of conflict when engaging with the child. I viewed these histories and feelings as impairing and strengthening my capacity to read the child's emotionally delivered words. Now I understand this kind of reading to resemble a method that is perhaps more Kleinian than the talking cure used in the cases of Freud. As with Klein, my interpretations departed from "figuring out" the meaning of the child's symbolic associations. I instead worked with the transference operating between myself and the emotional expression of the child-learner. I staged imaginary conversations with the inside of a child in conversation with her insides spoken painfully to me. I mined untold meaning from her novel constructions of self and others.

I was highly recognized by my teaching peers for demonstrating a nurturing method of pedagogical engagement that supported children to learn to their best ability. When asked for my method, I was reluctant to share insight. I was afraid to expose myself to professional ridicule. Deep down inside, I knew my capacity for teaching did not come from teacher education. It came from a fairly canonical English education that forced me to sustain engagement with novels. I learned how to teach from communing with a novelist's communications rumbling in fabulous literary creations. In the classroom, I read children's communication as I do fiction. I followed the unfathomable emotional content of children in their novel expression. I studied the child's difficulties with symbols as a problem of the word's ability to be meaningful to her rather than as a problem of cognition. I encouraged children to make up words when they could not find one that felt right.

My administrators viewed me as a teacher possessing a "gift for teaching." But, again, for me the capacity was not innate: my gift for teaching came directly from a childhood of stories written in my parents' second language and emotionally delivered in an immigrant's conflict-held words. I did not know their language but I understood the significance of their narratives. It is difficult to explain how one can make meaning of words one cannot literally decode. For this, one needs a theory of language that exceeds words, a theory of literacy of more than just words. To this day, I cannot fluently speak or read and write in my mother's language. I might never learn to read and write in the tongue of my mother, to read the life-giving words of Tagore or of news of the homeland in a newspaper. An inhibited capacity to learn my mother tongue continues to bear witness to my traumatic, forced entry into English.

English severed our mother's tongue. Still, all was not lost when I lost my mother tongue. Her loss persisted in the cadence of a broken-down English rooted inside my compulsive efforts to speak my mind. Productive and ruined relations with my mother tongue support a creative and generative emotional capacity for English. This remarkable childhood capacity, bent toward interpretation rather than understanding, was restored and altered when I was made to read and make sense of hundreds of novels in university. Unable to comply with the professor's interpretation of novels, I found myself alone in literary thoughts, grappling with the secret content of the other, and unable to share my view. Still and stubbornly, I held my interpretations tightly to my heart. I kept them close to my teaching and wore my wild readings on my sleeve. And then, magically and incredibly, in the classroom with children my felt literary thought became of use, my felt readings found a home in the inner worlds and imaginations of children.

Where I am tempted to cite Shakespeare as giving me my first entry into poetic form, I cite my Bengali mother, who never learned to speak proper English. Her strange yet potent use of language supported me in my supporting the literacy of emergent and second language learners in my classroom. It helped me read novels from the inside out. My improper English taught me to read and write as if my survival, and those of my students, depended on it.

Not unlike Jackie Derrida who wanted to speak and write proper French, I also became a powerful speaker and writer of English. If my English was neither standard nor proper, it was good enough to survive among native and other recently admitted Canadian lyrical and nonconforming English speakers. Ironically, and very unlike the masterful and highly distinguished French writer, my repeated failures to communicate, as a child and later as an English scholar, strengthened my capacity for felt interpretation. I continue to struggle to communicate in commanding, standard, lucid prose my findings of the world. And yet the meanings and workings of the mind are not completely made evident in words. Communicable evidence of literacy only tells a very small part of the incredibly plastic and elusive human mind story. Left waiting and wanting in these cognitive and brain-based theories, is the person and experience behind words, beneath words, inside words, making and made of words.

The novel readings I offer in this book are provocative. My findings are counterintuitive to the work of educational psychologists and scholars of literacy and literature. These fictions show language acquisition and use to be animated by what drives form as well as content. These novel constructions of the infantile, inner, and reparative potential of literacy offer an invitation to others to think anew and deeply about literacy. If these insights compel in readers a second reading, a second consideration of the existential significance of literacy in their own lives, it will be enough. If teachers begin to read novels to support their teaching, it will be enough. Engaging our worded triumphs, conflicts, and failures as speakers, readers, writers, and scholars, we are gifted with training in a literacy of the Other. This literacy is attuned to the felt and unique experience of human beings buried beneath their words. When we are open to the idea that communication is difficult and that knowledge is predicated on uncertainty and taking a chance to say something, we are given insight into the joy and pain of using words to give voice to our internal and external realities and those of others.

In *Humanism of the Other*, Emmanuel Lévinas suggests that a hyper-narcissistic orientation toward the self has led to unthinkable consequences for scapegoated and dehumanized "Others" of the world. Lévinas suggests, quite radically, that from birth we are for the other, given to the other, existing only for and by the mercy of others. The thought of the Other helps us find faith in our precarious beginnings: our imagined belief in the Other supports us to live. Lévinas insists that to repay this existential debt to a (m)other outside ourselves we might orient ourselves to others. And he cites language, our capacities and use, as key to this ethical orientation, an orientation that he insists begins at birth and childhood with our mother.

Along with being other-oriented, I position literacy in this book as a novel experience—a felt and fictive experience of renewal that compels the tiny prelingual human to find and form words to create and convey the essence of her self to others. Our problem with communication is ours for a lifetime. We need literacy, a symbolic communicative structure, across the life span. Literacy takes a leading role in our mental, physical, and emotional capacities to develop and grow. As the child takes in and uses words to communicate, she learns to narrate herself with stories inherited from adults. Literacy in adult stories supports her to symbolically imagine, communicate, and narrate herself to others.

One's need for and use of literacy corresponds with different stages of one's emotional, physical, and social development. In infancy, we depend on the mother's words to make our existence recognizable. In childhood, we need words to forge incredible experiments with the world and others. In adolescence, we need words to break free from the normative binds of familial relations to risk and find new social ties, to risk and write new narratives of the self (Gilbert, 2007). In midlife, we can find our self in crisis, as faith in the power of words to master the world wanes, as we are faced with lost youth, grown children, dying friends and parents, and thoughts of death. At the end of our lives we again become dependent on the other's words, as we were in infancy, straining for others to represent our lives to their indignant end. Literacy, in its radical existential sense is not simply mastered, and once consolidated, exploited and abandoned. Literacy is given to the child to story an entire life in search of meaning. As the child learns these stories she is inserted into her place in a family, a history, and a world. A reception and revision of stories accompanies our formation as people throughout our lifetime. The pedagogical processes by which literacy stories and is storied by grand normative narratives of development bolster, support, hinder, and ruin a person's potential to become someone in the world. In this regard, my book contributes a radical understanding of literacy as key to one's capacity to form, narrate, and renew their personhood across a lifetime of becoming someone. Fostering an attention to the work of literacy in the lifespan can teach human beings to live with meaning, less violently and with creative possibility.

Klein (1930) conceptualizes language as evident in the child's impassioned efforts to bridge internal, symbolic, and external worlds. Her analytic constructs produced from her incredibly sympathetic readings of the child's emotional life are at the heart of my conceptualization of literacy. Klein took the child's internal symbolic capacity to make existential meaning as her guide for analysis. She focused on how children made meaningful attachments to object-others through fabulous linguistic formations. From her sustained efforts with the inner worlds of children emerged a theory of language bolstered by the child's propensity for fantasy and fiction. She located the child's literary capacity in her emotional core. My readings of both children and novels are immersed in the emotional content of symbolic formation. Following unspeakable affect as shaky witness to the untold meaning in words, we can learn how to read for the inner life of symbolic formation. The lessons learned from aesthetic engagements in literature are instructive in a pedagogy of literacy.

Literacy is animated and fueled by the emotional material of the learner's inner world. Infantile symbolization and the novelist's affective-aesthetic craft are animated by an other and are given form in the author's novel formations. Those of us who are compelled to read and sustain a critical engagement with novels do so because literature taps into our emotional, inner lives where the phantasy child still resides. Sendak's Max is a phantasy child; he represents our feelings of childhood necessarily, and at times miserably, subject to the words of adults. To qualify these feelings, Max offers both children and adults a dream work vision of "the rumpus of the wild things." This "real" story of the wild forms of life taken by our upset feelings helps us take stock and comfort; Sendak's well-placed and chosen words console and make new our own.

Exemplary literature builds ups in the child a vast repertoire of words with which to think a felt existence. We read novels to make meaning of our lives through the words of another just as the infant is compelled to read her mother's words to make sense of her strange existential condition. Both situations are highly charged. Reading can be a somewhat frustrating experience where one wordlessly communicates with another a shared, but in vastly different versions, story of felt significance. In this novel communication across difference, writer and reader co-construct a fiction that each has yet to completely understand.

Coleman (2009) suggests that reading is paradoxical because it is a solitary yet relational activity. Derrida insists this paradox is not simply given to reading but grounds a fictional human existence phantastically initiated in infancy by a pressing need to read and be read by a (m)other. We are born with a dire need of the other's language to make our unfathomable insides lovable, recognizable, communicable to others. This existential fact gives us grief and possibility: "I have a language, yet it is not mine" (Derrida 1998, 2).

As the infant clamors to make her needs known from the potent but grief-limited symbolic resource of crying, the mother creates of her affect a narrative of personality of the baby. The baby's story is constructed in the meaning or lack of meaning of words held in a mother's care and comfort. We depend on this affective relational narrative of existence to be made recognizable. Later, we depend on our mother's symbolic narrative of ourselves to tentatively and publicly renarrate ourselves, to make known our shaky thoughts and ideas of ourselves to others, to create fabulous institutions, to enact care and justice toward others. Learning to read the grand and socialized familial narrative can also be impoverished and hurtful to a lived sense of self. Some stories told of our self wound or betray our sense of belonging. Some stories break us down and weaken our resolve. Some stories find us on our knees begging for reprieve. But we need the other's words even as they break our hearts and tear us apart. Renarrating ourselves is also the means by which we repair and renew representations that fail to do justice to our lives—perhaps the most powerful form of literacy is creative word work, which labors, through the work of mourning, to repair meaning and renew significance, to remake out of the other's ruinous words a story of our own.

Reading novels, we yearn for a second chance to make meaning of our lives through a (m)other that seems actually reachable to an adult, literate self. Equipped with the capacity to symbolically communicate we can depend on the other's fictional news of a big wide world to metabolize old and yet to be told stories of our self in renewed form. A lifetime ago, I first read Derrida's memoir accounting for his struggles with the language of French. I found myself transported to the painful memories of childhood of a little boy in Algeria struggling to speak in school. The version of a tiny person's existence he offered, overcame my own. Filled with grief and gratitude, I left his story with renewed possibility for my lost mother tongue, for myself, for my mind, for my writing. The affect of Derrida's words struck me at the very core, sticking to me still, though I do not know (how to read) this person, a person whose fabulous ideas of writing continue to grace my mind and life. For two and a half decades, I am affected by my in-mind encounter with a person I have never met. I read and read his words, still "grubbing after the roots" to know why (Coetzee 2003).

Reading affects us over a lifetime of words. Our reading for ontic significance can remind us of the difficulty of existence. The novel invites us into a communal space of humility and deep introspection.

The inner space allows the reader to bear witness to her own thoughts in relation to words and ideas put forth by another. Suspended in the "psychic event of reading," we are offered a chance to reconsider the significance of the other's words in our lives (Robertson 1999). Reading can also offer a placeholder for our frustrations with the other's words. In a novel, we can fantastically act out feelings of destruction by destroying the other's words without actually hurting the other. From reading, we learn how to better sublimate and contain ourselves when affected by the other's words and presence. And through our productive and destructive reading and rereadings of the other's thoughts, we can be changed.

The demeaning formulation of literacy, as the means by which humanization is tautologically and instrumentally achieved, haunts Burroughs's incredible fiction as well as those educational and "scientific" fictions underpinning schooled practices of literacy. As with this novel, our profound fall into language as infants is divorced from our formal education. It is also, curiously, erased from academic and popular accounts of literacy. At best, developmental theories mark intelligent thought at six months, at the moment of speaking. We continue to view preverbal, infant communication or "any language we cannot understand" as a kind of ape language (Riviere in Klein et al. 1952, 20). Children who show delayed or different linguistic expressions are deemed to be developmentally or cognitively delayed. These children, prone to using silence, emotion, guttural responses, and gestures to communicate, are deemed savage, presymbolic, and thus not quite human. Teachers still equate English literacy with a modern, and now globally, advancing human status (Tarc 2013).

A theory of literacy as given to the self by other, recognizes that language depends upon ontic narratives and becomes inert when presented as an isolated set of skills detached from a human story. Rather than simply be used to read and write a narrative, our forms of literacy, and the assumptions literacy holds, in the first place produces the story. Lear (2002) refers to the fantastic stories we create to bolster and triumph human existence as core ontological narratives. And he suggests that these triumphant narratives foreclose the less glorious story of a "family of limitations that characterize the human condition" (Lear 2006, 119). In this untold story we are not all-powerful, words cannot save of us from ourselves, we cannot conquer or change the world, and we desperately need our (m)other (Farley and Mishra Tarc, 2014). English literacy provides us with an ontic frame of mind that has produced a version of superior, perfect, and progressive modern family life. This story is ideal, remarkable, even desirable. But this story is also a fabulous fiction that does not hold for those it dehumanizes. When reoriented as a novel experience, literacy falters in making certain claims to human existence. As a fictive experience, literacy is no longer evidence of a self-contained mind hardwired with the power of cognition and given to reason. Literacy is instead an animated, psychosocial and co-constructed experience, one indebted to the infant's clamoring effort to creatively make her self known to an other.

Reorienting Literacy: Return to Infancy

In this study, I offer a story of literacy, which acknowledges the uncertainties of its shaky beginning. Our unique internal mechanisms for making sense of the world shape our reading practices. These mechanisms are constructed out of one's most formative and felt experience with (m)others. As the child develops, she replaces the internal world's objects with the external world's words. Literacy imposes upon the child's unique mental processes another, and as I repeatedly imply, nonintuitive and instrumental system for symbolic meaning making. It teaches her that uncertain meanings can be replaced (captured) with words that name. Our internal processing system does not match evenly on to our external processes for reading and writing. At times, the two systems are horribly out of sync. Language serves, somewhat unreliably, as the mediator between the two (Coetzee 2003). Language is given the task of having to narrate two warring systems with vastly different ontological consequences. Somewhere in the clash of these two worlds (inner and external) comes knowledge (of both).

Many educators are uncomfortable with the uncertainties of learning, as evidenced by their fixating on objectives, outcomes, evidence, and measures. Most formal efforts go into finding and mandating the best way, the right way, the most (cost-) effective and efficient way to learn. Accordingly, Britzman notes, the educational enterprise shows little doubt "towards its own motivations and goals":

> Our educational efforts may not have a theory of the inner world or of emotional life. Second, given that mainstream education is so enamored by brain theory and theories of cognition, resistance to thinking of emotional life as the

> grounds for thinking itself—both from the perspective of the teacher and student—is even left unthought. And third, the chilling effects of the testing industry contribute to an instrumental, repressive orientation to knowledge. The procedures of content, comprehension, and skills dominate pedagogical interactions, and there is hardly time for curiosity into the mysteries of being. (Britzman 2006c, 169)

As Britzman indicates, educators presently face great challenges in fostering a literacy that honors and responds to the inner life and mysteries of existence of students. Perhaps the obstacles are too formidable: there is no time, there is too much to cover, there are too many students with social problems. Postmodern and neoliberal cultures of performativity (Lyotard 1984) only intensify the demands for outcomes and measurement, especially as an issue of equality (Tarc 2013). Moreover, educational research on literacy remains bound to its foundation in theories of cognition and brain theory. It is also tied to ontological theories of being and to the myth of the all-knowing subject. Our obsessive love of reason ensures that the emotional life be black-boxed. A return to psychoanalysis, with its literary construction of the inner life, offers a way forward—or backward to move forward. Freud's work can be a critical resource for framing a theory of learning and literary pedagogy. Still, I suspect that too many of us are taught to distrust Freud and his "dangerous" stories.

Thinking of the emotional life as the grounds of thinking is not a "celebration" of emotion in the classroom, as the current overemphasis on "feeling good" or fostering self-esteem in classrooms might imply. Nor is it a deferral of sophisticated theory. In the context of this study, thinking of emotional life in the classroom involves considering the relationship children make between their inner worlds and language. It involves reading theory as if it too were a grand story we tell to "nourish our selves" with a life of meaning (Phillips 2000).

Klein brilliantly staked her theory of what words can mean in the inner world of young children. She told stories of the child's emotional states and behaviors ripe with insight into the internal world's mechanisms at work. Klein read the dreamy minds of children in the behaviors they exhibited at play. She searched for mysteries of the internal world surfacing in the child's chatter, frequent outbursts, incessant questions, imaginative play, and obsessions with body parts, food, and toilet-talk. Her clinical method required sustained one-to-one engagement with children. She stayed with and thought through their feelings and actions. She engaged these feelings and actions through directed talk or the question. And she privileged the child's articulations over her own in the sense that her theories were based on what they told her. She took this secret knowledge as her guide when reworking existing Freudian theories of psychic development.

Literacy is bound to the child's compulsion to communicate. This learning predates school. It is laid down in the baby's mind in a maternally rendered scene. The scene of infancy actively haunts subsequent pedagogies of language learning. Heather Price writes:

> It can be difficult for literate adults to hold in mind how complex a process literacy learning might be developmentally. It can also be hard to recover a sense of what it is like to undergo this often slow and faltering learning process, the process of working out how to make meaning from text. (2005, 46)

As with the pain of any labor, once over, one cannot remember the qualities of that earlier activity. For this reason, theories of literacy need to be informed by a sustained (experiential) engagement with young children at home and in the classroom. Primary caregivers play a foundational role in the literacy education of children. Their practices deserve as much researching as those of professional teachers.

Our practices of literacy should also take into account the historical relationship the marginalized have with the dominant symbolic order. Too much emphasis has been placed on the difficulty some children pose for the school system rather than the difficulty that dominant systems and languages pose for children. Educational problems are situated in a larger historical context, and literacy teachers are obligated to consider a modern history of language education that dehumanizes the lives of children. Dehumanizing forms of language demean the child and also her family and community. As Oliver (2002) repeatedly points out, language teaches those excluded from dominant society that their inner and lived realities cannot be given to words that matter. Without just representation, subaltern realities struggle to exist (Spivak 1988).

Altering our story takes place one reading at a time with our entry into the language of others. Changing how we have learned to be, Freud (1937) reminds me, is much more difficult than learning to be. It is impossible to eradicate the law of words—it is the order of thinking by which Western thought operates. All language operates according to an order, a law that by definition colonizes others. The colonized colonize. We use language to colonize others in our family and in school. And even as we eradicate one form of violence or cruelty, another cruelty will be there to replace it—and perhaps with more terror and tenacity (Derrida 1989). We have to inhabit and bear the violence we commit to others to potentially lessen and sublimate violence we do to ourselves and to others. Symbolically responding to violence is not easy. It requires imaginative responses and experimental thinking and a speculative language that can repair and renew.

Renarrating Humanity: Literacy of the Other

> Stories matter.
> Many stories matter.
> Stories have been used to dispossess and to malign,
> but stories can also be used to empower and to humanize.
> Stories can break the dignity of a people,
> but stories can also repair that broken dignity.
> Chimamanda Adichie (2009 17:24–17:44)

In her Ted Talk lecture the Nigerian novelist Chimamanda Adichie cites the power of narrative in the formation of the life of a person and lives of a people. Drawing on her literate history, Adichie recounts the effects of English colonial education on her early literacy and consequently with herself and others. Immersed in stories of English men Adichie learned of the other's world, of the English countryside and ginger beer. But she was puzzled that throughout her education there was no story of her world. And as she made her way into the adult world she began to realize that without a story her world struggled to exist.

Adichie suggests that the pedagogy of literacy by which the child enters into a story of her world is important to her understanding of a world of others. Without negating the value of her English education, Adichie puts forth the idea that human existence is enriched and renewed by supporting the child's capacity to represent her self to others through multiple means and modes of literate practice. A new and hospitable world is remade with many stories of many lived realities of sentient beings struggling to coexist.

In this book, I take the position that that the child's capacity to use language is dependent on her adult caregivers and the historical and social context in which they reside. Language colonizes the child for better and for worse. Literacy is pedagogically delivered to the child in stories handed down, most often, in the voices of mothers, of teachers, of people with authority of the world. The patriarchal and colonizing existential effect of literacy is not an occasion for mass abandonment of the Word but an invitation to give painstaking and sustained thought to our continually evolving ideas, stories, and practices of literacy. Reorienting literacy to the maternal relation infuses our ongoing pedagogical practices of words with the uncertain, faltering emotional life of the child. In an other-oriented literacy, our teaching follows and supports the child's first readings of existential narratives, open to the promise and wonder of her words and the words of the world.

Gayatri Spivak (2004) insists that an altered literacy demands of us a literal rereading of what it means to be human. In this book, I extend this idea: a rereading of what it means to be *human* requires a literary rereading of what it means to be *literate*. We cannot afford to abandon aspects of institutionalized literacy but neither can we continue to practice literacy without thinking about the dominant forms of life it produces. In times when the novel is said to be dying or dead (Self 2014) and reading is on the wane (Coleman 2009), more urgent than ever is the need for a responsible and responsive literacy in the adult's pedagogically delivered narration of the child's stories of existence. The existential version of literacy poses the novel as an affectively worded production of a person's character, scene, plot line, and situation, rather than a mere man-made object of culture. A theory of literacy bound to existence is critical to the healthy, thoughtful, and less violent social formation of human subjects. In education we often focus on the effect of particular content and practices of teaching and learning on the subject formation of students (Willinsky 1998). Education is also the dominant means of shaping the desire of children through affective coercion to convince the child she wants the "gifts" culture promises (Spivak 2004). For both its promise and its power in sentient life we need to pay concerted attention to our pedagogies and practices of English literacy.

Novelists also emphasize the importance of creating and weaving multiple possible and impossible narratives to support the life of a person and people. Narrative is more than a story we tell about other people. Storied representation is also a dominant co-relational means by which the instantiation of desire and power materializes in the existential realities of sentient beings. A different story of a person or a people requires a different literate practice, one in which the adult attends to the infinite possibilities teeming in the life of the newly arrived child in a preformed world. We might gain lessons from late modernist novelists featured in this book, possessed with an empyrean capacity to embark on imaginative literate practices that attend to the fictional distance between the self and other. Novel engagements are key to renewing complex, intertwining narratives of human coexistence.

In Klein's (1937) essay on reparation, she insists that to make relations with others we need to make relations with ourselves. Relations are not simply attachments but the communication of those attachments into a story with which we can live. Our story needs to be one of relations with our many selves and the others in those selves. Because we have been taught that the self is unified, we are under the illusion that we exist separately from others. Because most of us do not experience consciousness in tension, except in times of anxiety, we imagine ourselves whole. And this seems necessary for good mental and emotional health. But if we can bear imagining the tension, we can also see ourselves as continuously in conflict as each self jealously bids for our attention, each self competes to be heard, each self has a story to tell.

As I suggested in my readings of *Elizabeth Costello* and *Beloved*, the struggle for meaning that we experience every day in our interactions with others should signal to us that language is an unreliable mediator of our perceptions, thoughts, others, and world. Language can and does get it wrong. It cannot hear what our inner worlds are saying and it continually interferes with what the other is saying. But we need a common language to translate our thoughts back to the self and out to the other.

Britzman (2006b) finds that literature gives us pause from habituated frameworks of mind. Novels afford us a retreat from our pressing social reality. Novels invite us to simultaneously engage past and present selves and past and present others in the act of reading. Our experiences with literature provide an archive of existential thinking—a communion of our own and the other's thinking. When we write of those experiences we can gain perspective on what it is we think we are reading and how it is that we read. And we can be surprised at what we find.

In his final interview, conducted in the midst of dying, Derrida (2004) poignantly remarks that individuals are only *beginning to read* him. The grief in his sentence is hard to bear given that his incredible array of texts engaged the minds of thousands, of millions, and altered the course and conduct of Western thought. But of course Derrida is not talking about his books as objects. He is not even talking about his legacy or impact. He is not talking of the self but of the other. Reading is as communing with the writer's thoughts and experience, as acknowledging the human being behind the thinking, as recognizing the existence of a tiny, grief-stricken person struggling to speak. But beginning to read Derrida is still reading—first reading is the most profound reading we are given. It is a gift. Here the other meets our faltering communication with an attentive and nonassimilating response to sustain our existence. At a first reading we may not hear what the other labors to say. With a second and third reading we might get closer to the truth. Derrida's practice of literary poeisis against easy representation gives us this gift because he compels us to read and respond to him again and again. This is the only way to do justice to the Other; to read, reread, and respond to her infinitely (Lévinas 1969).

My first reading is of suffering. My mother, displaced from her family and perpetually homesick, told me stories about her lost parents and siblings left behind in West Bengal. She sorrowfully retold her motherland beginnings in a deeply affective and invented language—a half-English, half-Bengali hard-to-read language. I struggled with the words, but I heard and took in the sorrow. I suspect my readings continue to be influenced by competing versions of this originary and transferred sorrow. Perhaps this is why in times of loss I reach for a book.

Our institutions are founded on the ontological assumptions we transform into law to house the bodies of others. We, as human players, are invested in these institutions to support and preserve all of our ways of life. Yet, we have to reread our institutions by a different story of being, of a mother's sorrow or the baby's cry, in order to imagine, create, and support a meaningful existence of human being. A certain study of language, literature, theory, and pedagogical practice might provoke praxes of rereading human relations with and against self-preserving institutions. Pedagogically attending to the child's imaginative capacity to symbolize and story a self in relation to others might provide the basis for renarrating humanity. In this renewed story of a differently shared humanity the child is given to the soft and soothing words of (m)other and the world marked by the vicissitudes of suffering and pleasure, dependence and agency, creativity and decay. Literacy dependent on the nurturing words of the Other might then be put to use to reorient a heartbroken humanity toward renarrating a potentially reparative and novel story of our shared other-oriented existence.

Notes

Introduction

1. According to Kristeva (1987), the "loving third" mediates the relationship between mother and child. Kristeva conceives of the third as the "imaginary father." Oliver inserts the social/language or "loving support" in the place of the father to disrupt the dominant assumption that patriarchy is the only possible structure for sociality.

2. Throughout this book, I use *other* as its common usage, *Other* as signifying radical alterity, and *"Other"* as the metaphysical other. Other (no capital and no scare quotes) refers to the word's ordinary meaning as other than me.

3. Throughout this book, I use *mother* to refer to the historical and actual mother and *(m)other* to refer to a formative, caregiving other that may or may not be the biological mother. Mother refers to the infant-bearing, female, biological parent. (M)other refers to the infant's primary attachment with a significant other.

Chapter 1. Fictive Readings

1. I prefer the term *psychical* rather than *psychic* although psychoanalytic literature uses the latter. I find that in the field of education, psychic gets confused with the activities of mind reading or reading the future. The term *psychical* also lends itself more to a quality of mind rather than a state of mind, which is helpful in regard to my study of processes of the mind in literacy.

2. *Object* refers to the thing (breast), its invested meanings, and the interpretive psychosocial processes we bring to it.

3. Klein unconventionally spells fantasy with "ph" to signal that this process is unconscious. Phantasy is not to be confused with the social form of daydreaming or the literary genre—although these fictional spaces can give us insight into the infant's capacity to engage in terrifying and incredible spaces of preverbal "thinking." Phantasy is instead an unknowable and affective

mental state of the infant that expresses itself through the force and form of the baby's intense and pathetic efforts to communicate.

4. Much is made of the similarities between Lacan's theory of signification and Derrida's deconstruction. Although only hinted at in this book, I find that Derrida's concept of deconstruction forges a departure from Lacan's claim that the unconscious is structured like a language. Derrida's notion of trace in thinking deeply resembles Klein's theory of symbolization grounded in unconscious material and expressed in child's play. Derrida's seminal essay "Structure, Sign and Play in the Discourse of the Human Sciences" resounds in Klein's "play technique" and in his deconstruction of the great books of Western philosophy. In the fields of philosophy and psychoanalysis, a link is yet to be made between Derrida's deconstruction and Klein's theory of object relations.

5. Lacan's (2006) theory of subjectivity depends on vision following dominant metaphysical theories of subjectivity. It is when the child sees that she is apart from the mother that her self-determination begins. Following Klein (1928), I suggest that the baby hears her difference in the other's foreign sounds; difference is heard before seen.

Chapter 3. Projecting Humanity

1. Donna Haraway (1984) notes that Burroughs's representations of animals and women are often conflated or intermingled or equated, both figuratively, in the case of the images of miscegenation given off by the rape of Lady Greystoke by the apes, and literally, as in the case of Kala, the mother-ape. Burroughs also strategically depicts the white mother as pure and virginal and the ape or black mother as animalistic but instinctively maternal. In *Beloved*, Morrison also highlights this disturbing tendency in European/American thought to liken Africans to animals.

2. As with this example, the ape-language is consistently glossed by Burroughs in English translation. The glossing of other languages is a dominant feature of contemporary "postcolonial" literary novels written in English.

3. See Britzman's *After Education* (2003) for a comprehensive discussion of these reactions to Klein.

Chapter 4. Inside Reading

1. Costello reacts most intensely to the scenes of sadism in West's novel.

2. West's presence combined with Costello's travel to the conference (also body-altering) produces the memory. In his essay, *A Disturbance of Memory*

on the Acropolis, Freud (1936) implies that traveling can temporarily disorient and take one out of oneself, opening the self to new insights.

Chapter 5. Healing Language

1. I take Juliet Mitchell's articulation for my definition of trauma: "A trauma, whether physical or psychical, must create a breach in a protective covering of such severity that it cannot be coped with by the usual mechanisms by which we deal with pain or loss. . . . Whether it is as childhood seduction, infantile abuse, shell shock, or war violence, or as a preoccupation with the place of neoteny and the trials of human birth, trauma is continually posited as the hypothetical 'origin' of psychic states. . . . Psychoanalysis is equipped to contribute to the understanding of the *reaction* to trauma, not to the trauma itself" (1998, 121; italics added). As Mitchell indicates, trauma itself resists representation; representation of trauma can deepen or lessen suffering, can illuminate or defend against meaning.

2. And, I would add, psychical consequences. Dean Franco writes: "Morrison consistently twins the language of spiritual and psychic devastation with the language of material loss and legal injury, giving us a materially textured surface that conforms to the depths of the spirit" (2006, 428).

3. In the preface to later editions of the novel, Morrison writes: "The historical Margaret Garner is fascinating, but, to a novelist, confining. Too little imaginative space there for my purposes. So I would invent her thoughts, plumb them for a subtext that was historically true in essence, but not strictly factual in order to relate her history to contemporary issues about freedom, responsibility and woman's 'place' " (2004, xvii).

4. As with other reductive categories of identity, Morrison's depiction of whiteness is not limited to her representation of Schoolteacher or the nephews. As with depictions of milk, the tree, and the Word, Morrison continually plays with multiple meanings of White circulating across a number of discourses. Sethe's relationship of ethical singularity with Amy Denver (after whom she names her daughter) and the compassion Sethe experiences from the Garners starkly contrasts her experience with Schoolteacher.

5. Derrida (1978a) describes "finite silence" as annihilating the trace/voice of the other (118).

6. The Word is the Word of God upon which the slaves and ex-slaves once depended to find meaning for their lives. Baby Suggs depends on the Word in her sermons summoning the ex-slaves to their former selves. However, as I have demonstrated with other symbols, Morrison plays on the different significations of the Word (as "thing," as Law, as inscription, as meaning making)

to open up and resituate meanings of symbolic law and force the reader to grapple with the Word's multiple significations and significance.

7. This fragment, "language there all along" refers to the maternal language of Sethe's mother. The whole quote is as follows: "What Nan told her she had forgotten, along with the language she told it in. The same language her ma'am spoke, and which would never come back. But the message—that was and had been there all along" (Morrison 2004, 74). The passage also refers to the traumatic journey of newly captured slaves, Sethe's grandmother (Nan) and her mother, making their way from Africa to America. During the journey, Sethe's mother is forced to "throw" all of her children but Sethe out of the boat. Morrison links together several past events in the effects of transgenerational trauma. Significantly, these effects are transferred from one generation of *women* to the next (mothers to daughters).

Bibliography

Adichie, C. 2009. "The Danger of a Single Story." Ted Talk. Accessed November 13. http://www.ted.com/talks/chimamanda_adichie_the_danger_of_a_single_story.html.

Angelo, B., and T. Morrison. 1989. "The Pain of Being Black." *Time*, May 22. Accessed April 7. http://www.time.com/time/community/pulitzerinterview.html.

Arendt, H. 2006. "The Crisis of Education." In *Between Past and Present*. New York: Penguin.

Attridge, D. and Baldwin, T. 2004. Jacques Derrida. *The Guardian*, March 11. Accessed November 12. http://www.theguardian.com/news/2004/oct/11/guardianobituaries.france.

Bhabha, H. K. 1994. *The Location of Culture*. London: Routledge.

Bollas, C. 1999. *The Mystery of Things*. London: Routledge.

Britzman, D. P. 1995. "Is There a Queer Pedagogy? Or Stop Thinking Straight." *Educational Theory* 45, no. 2: 151–65.

———. 2000. "If the Story Cannot End: Deferred Action, Ambivalence, and Difficult Knowledge." In *Between Hope and Despair: Pedagogy and the Representation of Historical Trauma*, edited by R. Simon. S. Rosenberg, and C. Eppert. 27–58. Lanham, MD: Rowman and Littlefield.

———. 2003. *After-Education: Anna Freud, Melanie Klein, and Psychoanalytic Histories of Learning*. Albany: State University of New York Press.

———. 2006a. *Novel Education: Psychoanalytic Studies of Learning and Not Learning*. New York: Peter Lang.

———. 2006b. "On Being a Slow Reader: Psychoanalytic Reading Problems in Ishiguro's *Never Let Me Go*." *Changing English* 13, no. 3: 307–18.

———. 2006c. "Sigmund Freud, Melanie Klein, and Little Oedipus: On the Pleasures and Disappointments of Sexual Enlightenment. In *Love's Return: Psychoanalytic Essays on Childhood, Teaching, and Learning*, edited by G. Boldt, P. Salvio, and Amy Mapes, 165–84. New York: Routledge.

———. 2009a. *The Very Thought of Education. Psychoanalysis and the Impossible Professions*. Albany: State University of New York Press.

———. 2009b. "Love's Impression: A Psychoanalytic Contribution." *British Journal of Sociology of Education* 30, no. 6: 773–87.

———, and A. J. Pitt. 1996. "Pedagogy and Transference: Casting the Past of Learning into the Presence of Teaching." *Theory into Practice* 35, no. 2: 117–23.

Burroughs, E. R. 1939 (1990). *The Adventures of Lord Greystoke: Tarzan of the Apes*. Toronto: Random House.

Casey, K. 1990. "Teacher as Mother. Curriculum Theorizing in the Life Histories of Contemporary Women Teachers." *Cambridge Journal of Education* 20: 301–20.

Celan, P. 2001. *Selected Poems and Prose of Paul Celan*. Translated by J. Felstiner. New York: W. W. Norton.

Cheyfitz, E. 1997. *The Poetics of Imperialism: Translation and Colonization from The Tempest to Tarzan*. Philadelphia: University of Pennsylvania Press.

Chomsky, N. 1975. *The Logical Structure of Linguistic Theory*. New York: Plenum Press.

Coetzee, J. M. 1986. *Foe*. London: Secker and Warburg.

———. 1999. *The Lives of Animals*. Princeton: Princeton University Press.

———. 2000. *Disgrace*. London: Vintage.

———. 2003. *Elizabeth Costello*. New York: Viking.

———. 2007. "A Word from J. M. Coetzee. Voiceless: I Feel Therefore I Am." Unpublished lecture. Sidney, Australia: Sherman Gallery.

Coleman, D. 2009. *In Bed with the Word. Reading, Spirituality, and Cultural Politics*. Edmonton: University of Alberta Press.

Corliss, R. 1999. "Him Tarzan, Him great." *Time* Magazine, June 6. Accessed April 7. http://www.time.com/time/magazine/article/0,9171,991214,00.html?iid=chix-sphere.

Crichlow, W., and C. McCarthy. 1995. "Introduction: Toni Morrison and the Curriculum." *Cultural Studies* 9, no. 2: 205–209.

Cummings, J., V. Bismilla, P. Chow, S. Cohen, F. Giampapa, L. Leoni, P. Sandhu, and P. Sastri. 2005. "Affirming Identity in Multilingual Classrooms." *Educational Leadership* 63, no. 1: 38–43.

Darnton, R. 2001. "The History of Reading." In *New Perspectives of Historical Writing* edited by P. Burke, 157–86. New York: Polity Press.

Davies B. 1993. *Shards of Glass: Children Reading and Writing beyond Gendered Identities.* Cresskill, NJ: Hampton Press.

Denzin, N. K., and Y. S. Lincoln. 2000. *Handbook of Qualitative Research.* 2nd ed. Thousand Oaks, CA: Sage.

Derrida, J. 1976a. *Of Grammatology*. Translated by G. Spivak. Baltimore: Johns Hopkins University Press.

———. 1976b (1995). "Between Brackets I." In *Points . . . : Interviews, 1974–1994*, translated by P. Kamuf and edited by E. Weber, 5–29. Stanford: Stanford University Press.

———. 1978a. "Violence and Metaphysics: An Essay on the Thought of Emmanuel Lévinas." In *Writing and difference*, translated by A. Bass, 79–153. Chicago: University of Chicago Press.

———. 1978b. "Structure, Sign, and Play in the Discourse of the Human Sciences." In *Writing and Difference*, translated by A. Bass, 278–94. Chicago: University of Chicago Press.

———. 1981. "Economimesis." Translated by R. Klein. *Diacritics* 11, no. 2: 2–25.

———. 1982 (1995). "The Almost Nothing of the Unrepresentable." In *Points . . . : Interviews, 1974–1994*, translated by P. Kamuf and edited by E. Weber, 78–88. Stanford: Stanford University Press.

———. 1986. "Racism's Last Word." In *"Race," Writing, and Difference*, translated by P. Kamuf and edited by H. L. Gates and K. A. Appiah, 329–58. Chicago: University of Chicago Press.

———. 1989 (1995). "Eating Well, or the Calculation of the Subject." In *Points . . . : Interviews, 1974–1994*, translated by P. Kamuf and edited by E. Weber, 255–87. Stanford: Stanford University Press.

———. 1998. *Monolingualism of the Other, or, The Prosthesis of Origin*. Translated by P. Menash. Stanford: Stanford University Press.

———. 2002. "The Animal Therefore I Am (More to Follow)." Translated by D. Willis. *Critical Inquiry* 28, no. 2: 369–418.

———, and J. Bimbaum. 2004. "I Am at War with Myself." *Le Monde*, August 18. Accessed July 10. http://www.egs.edu/faculty/jacques-derrida/articles/i-am-at-war-with-myself/.

Dunlop, R. 2000. *Boundary Bay*. Winnipeg: Turnstone Press.

Edgerton, S. H. 1995. "Re-Membering the Mother Tongue(s): Toni Morrison, Julie Dash, and the Language of Pedagogy." *Cultural Studies* 9, no. 2: 338–63.

Eppert, C. 2000. "Relearning Questions: Responding to the Ethical Address of Past and Present Others." In *Between Hope and Despair. Pedagogy and the Remembrance of Historical Trauma*, edited by R. Simon, S. Rosenberg, and C. Eppert. 213–30. Lanham, MD: Rowman and Littlefield.

Fanon, F. 1967. *Black Skins. White Masks*. New York: Grove Press.

Farley, L. 2012. "An Essay Is Being Written: Between Aggression and 'Just Words.'" *Changing English* 19, no. 2: 167–78.

———, and A. Mishra Tarc. 2014. "Drawing Trauma: The Therapeutic Potential of Witnessing the Child's Visual Testimony of War." *Journal of the American Psychoanalytic Association* 62, no. 5: 835–54.

Felman, S., and D. Laub. 1992. *Testimony: Crises of Witnessing in Literature, Psychoanalysis, and History*. New York: Routledge.

Felstiner, J. 2001. "Preface." In *Selected poems and prose of Paul Celan*. xix–xxxvi. New York: W. W. Norton.

Fink, B. 1995. *The Lacanian Subject: Between Language and Jouissance*. Princeton: Princeton University Press.

Franco, D. 2006. "What We Talk about When We Talk about *Beloved*." *Modern Fiction Studies* 52, no. 2: 415–39.

Freebody, P., and A. Luke. 1990. "Literacies Programs: Debates and Demands in Cultural Context." *Prospect: Australian Journal of TESOL* 5, no. 7: 7–16.

Freire, P. 1982. *Pedagogy of the Oppressed*. New York: Continuum.

Freud, S. 1905. "Fragment of an Analysis of a Case of Hysteria." In *The Standard Edition of the Complete Psychological Works of Sigmund Freud, Volume VII (1901–1905): A Case of Hysteria, Three Essays on Sexuality, and Other Works*, translated and edited by J. Strachey, 1–122. New York: W. W. Norton.

———. 1909 (1977). "Analysis of a Phobia in a 5 Year Old Boy." In *Pelican Freud library, Vol 8, Case Histories*. New York: Pelican Books.

———. 1915 (1984). "Repression." In *On Metapsychology: The Theory of Psychoanalysis*. Vol. 11, translated by J. Strachey and edited by A. Richard, 139–58. London: Penguin Books.

———. 1917. "Mourning and Melancholia." In *The Standard Edition*. Vol. XIV, translated and edited by J. Strachey, 243–58. London: Hogarth.

———. 1920 (1984). "Beyond the Pleasure Principle." In *On Metapsychology: The Theory of Psychoanalysis*. Vol. 11, translated by J. Strachey and edited by A. Richard, 269–338. London: Penguin Books.

———. 1936 (1984). "A Disturbance of Memory on the Acropolis." In *On Metapsychology: The Theory of Psychoanalysis*. Vol. 11, translated by J. Strachey and edited by A. Richard, 443–56. London: Penguin Books.

———. 1937. "Analysis Terminable and Interminable." Translated by J. Riviere. *International Journal of Psycho-Analysis* 18: 373–405.

Gaines, E. J. 1993. *A Lesson before Dying*. New York: Alfred A. Knopf.

Gee, J. P. 2004. *Situated Language and Learning: A Critique of Traditional Schooling*. New York: Routledge.

Gilbert, J. 2004. "Literature as Sex Education." *Changing English* 11, no. 2: 233–41.

———. 2007. "Risking a Relation: Sex Education and Adolescent Development. *Sex Education: Sexuality, Society and Learning* 7, no. 1: 47–61.

Giroux, H. 1990. "Reading Texts, Literacy, and Textual Authority." *Journal of Education* 172, no. 1: 84–103.

Green, A. 1999. *The Fabric of Affect in the Psychoanalytic Discourse*. Translated by A Sheridan. London: Routledge.

———. 2008. *The Chains of Eros. The Sexual in Psychoanalysis*. Translated by L. Thurston. London: Karnac Books.

Greene, M. 1995. *Releasing the Imagination: Essays on Education, the Arts, and Social Change*. San Francisco: Jossey-Bass.

Grimes, W. 1993. "Toni Morrison Is '93 Winner of Nobel Prize in Literature. *New York Times*, October 8. Accessed April 7. http://www.nytimes.com/books/98/01/11/home/28957.html?_r=1&oref=slogin.

Grumet, M. R. 1988. *Bitter Milk: Women and Teaching*. Amherst: University of Massachusetts Press.

Gunew, S. 2001. "Technologies of Self: Corporeal Affects of English." *The South Atlantic Quarterly* 100, no. 3: 729–47.

Haraway, D. J. 1984. "Primatology is Politics by Other Means." *PSA: Proceedings of the Biennial Meeting of the Philosophy of Science Association*, 489–524.

Ishiguro, K. 2006. *Never Let Me Go*. London: Vintage.

Jacobus, M. 1999. *Psychoanalysis and the Scene of Reading*. Oxford: Clarendon.

Kamuf, P. 2000. "The Ends of Reading." Paper presented at the *Book/Ends* Conference, University of Alabama. Accessed April 7. http://www-rcf.usc.edu/~kamuf/text.html.

Kellner, D. 2004. "Technological Transformation, Multiple Literacies, and the Re-visioning of Education." *E-learning* 1, no. 1: 9–37.

Kendrick, M. 2011. "Playing House: A Sideways Glance at Literacy and Identity in Early Childhood." In *Major Works in Early Childhood Literacy*, edited by K. Pahl and J. Rowsell. Thousand Oaks, CA: Sage.

Kennedy, R. M. 2011. "Towards a Cosmopolitan Curriculum of Forgiveness." *Curriculum Inquiry* 41, no. 3: 373–93.

Klein, M. 1926 (1984). "The Psychological Principles of Early Analysis." In *Love, Guilt, and Reparation, and Other Works, 1921–1945*. Vol. I, edited by R. Money-Kyrle, 128–38. New York: The Free Press.

———. 1928 (1987). "Early Stages of the Oedipus Conflict." In *The Selected Melanie Klein*, edited by J. Mitchell, 69–83. New York: The Free Press.

———. 1930 (1984). "The Importance of Symbol-Formation in the Development of the Ego." In *Love, Guilt, and Reparation, and Other Works, 1921–1945*. Vol. I, edited by R. Money-Kyrle, 219–32. New York: The Free Press.

———. 1935 (1987). "A Contribution to the Psychogenesis of Manic-Depressive states." In *The Selected Melanie Klein*, edited by J. Mitchell, 115–45. New York: The Free Press.

———. 1937 (1984). "Love, Guilt, and Reparation." In *Love, Guilt, and Reparation, and Other Works, 1921–1945*. Vol. I, edited by R. Money-Kyrle, 306–43. New York: The Free Press.

———. 1940 (1984). "Mourning and Its Relation to Manic-Depressive States." In *Love, Guilt, and Reparation, and Other Works, 1921–1945*. Vol. I, edited by R. Money-Kyrle, 344–69. New York: The Free Press.

———. 1946. "Notes on Some Schizoid Mechanisms." *International Journal of Psychoanalysis* 27: 99–110.

———. 1952 (1975). "On Observing the Behavior of Young Children." In *Envy and Gratitude and Other Works 1946–1963*, edited by R. Money-Kyrle, 94–121. London: Hogarth Press.

———. 1955 (1987). "The Psycho-Analytic Play Technique: Its History and Significance." In *The Selected Melanie Klein*, edited by J. Mitchell, 35–56. New York: The Free Press.

———. 1961. *Narrative of a Child Analysis. The Conduct of Psychoanalysis of Children as Seen in the Treatment of a Ten-Year-Old Boy*. New York: The Free Press.

———, P. Heimann, S. Issacs, and J. Riviere. 1952. *Developments in Psychoanalysis*. London: Hogarth.

Kohon, G. 2005. "Love in a Time of Madness." In A. Green and G. Kohon, *Love and Its Vicissitudes*, 41–84. London: Routledge

Kristeva, J. 1987. *Tales of Love*. Translated by L. S. Roudiez. New York: Columbia University Press.

———. 1992. *Black Sun. Depression and Melancholia*. Translated by L. S. Roudiez. New York: Columbia University Press.

———. 2001. *Melanie Klein*. Translated by R. Guberman. New York: Columbia University Press.

Lacan, J. 2006. *Écrits: The First Complete Edition in English*. Translated by B. Fink. New York: W. W. Norton.

Lear, J. 1999. *Open Minded. Working out the Logic of the Soul*. Cambridge: Harvard University Press.

———. 2002. "Jumping from the Couch. An Essay on Phantasy and Emotional Structure." *International Journal of Psychoanalysis* 83: 583–95.

———. 2006. "Radical Hope." In *Ethics in the Face of Cultural Devastation*. Cambridge: Harvard University Press.

Leggo, C. 2012. *Sailing in a Concrete Boat. A Teacher's Journey*. Rotterdam: Sense Publishers.

Lévinas, E. 1969. *Totality and Infinity: An Essay on Exteriority*. Translated by A. Lingis. Pittsburgh: Duquesne University Press.

———. 2003. *Humanism of the Other*. Translated by N. Poller. Urbana: University of Illinois Press.

Lewkovich, D. 2012. *Alone in the Classroom* as Limit-Case. Reading the Circulations of Emotion in Education as Provocative Psychic Interruption." *Curriculum Inquiry* 42, no. 4: 454–71.

Liscio, L. 1992. "*Beloved*'s Narrative: Writing Mother's Milk." *Tulsa Studies in Women's Literature* 11, no. 1: 31–46.

Love, H. 2007. *Feeling Backward. Loss and the Politics of Queer Theory*. Cambridge: Harvard University Press.

Luke A., and P. Freebody. 1999. "Further Notes on the Four Resources Model." Reading Online. Accessed July 13. http://www.readingonline.org/research/lukefreebody.html.

Lyotard, J. F. 1984. *The Postmodern Condition: A Report on Knowledge* Translated by G. Bennington and B. Massumi. Minneapolis: University of Minnesota Press.

———. 1991. *The Inhuman: Reflections on Time*. Translated by G. Bennington and R. Bowlby. Stanford: Stanford University Press.

———. 2002. "(Ex)citing Philosophy." In *Lyotard. Philosophy, Politics, and the Sublime*, edited by H. Silverman, 23–48. New York: Routledge.

McCarthy, C., and W. Crichlow. 1993. *Race, Identity, and Representation in Education*. New York: Routledge.

McCarthy, C., and G. Dimitriadis. 2000. "Art and the Postcolonial Imagination: Rethinking the Institutionalization of Third World Aesthetics and Theory." *Ariel. A Review of International Literature* 31, no. 1–2: 231–53.

Mitchell, J. 1998. "Trauma, Recognition, and the Place of Language." *Diacritics* 28, no. 4: 121–33.

Mishra Tarc, A. 2009. "Postcolonial Studies as Re-education: Lessons from J. M. Coetzee's *Disgrace*. In *Postcolonial Challenges in Education*, edited by R. Sintos Colomas, 195–216. New York: Peter Lang.

———. 2011. "Reparative Curriculum." *Journal of Curriculum Inquiry* 41, no. 3: 350–72.

Morrison, T. 1988. "Unspeakable Things Spoken: The African American Presence in American Literature." Paper presented at the Tanner Lectures On Human Values, University of Michigan. Electronic Version. Accessed April 7. http://www.tannerlectures.utah.edu/lectures/morrison90.pdf.

———. 2004. *Beloved: A Novel*. New York: Penguin.

Nouvet, C. 2003. "The Inarticulate Affect. Lyotard and Psychoanalytic Testimony." *Discourse* 1 and 2: 231–47.

Oliver, K. 2001. *Witnessing. Beyond Recognition*. Minneapolis: University of Minnesota Press.

———. 2002. "Psychic Space and Social Melancholy." In *Between the Psyche and the Social: Psychoanalytic Social Theory*, edited by K. Oliver and S. Edwin, 49–65. Lanham, MD: Rowman and Littlefield.

Osgood, K. 2013. Kafka for Kids. *New Yorker*. Accessed November 21. http://www.newyorker.com/online/blogs/books/2013/06/kafka-for-kids.html.

Peeters, B. 2012. *Derrida. A Biography.* New York: Polity Press.

Phillips, A. 1999. *The Beast in the Nursery. On Curiosity and Other Appetites.* London: Vintage.

———. 2000. *Promises, Promises: Essays on Literature and Psychoanalysis.* London: Faber.

Price, H. 2005. "Lufta, a 'Slow' Learner: Understanding School Literacy Learning in Its Social and Emotional Context." *Infant Observation* 8, no. 1: 45–57.

Rich, A. C. 1993. *What Is Found There: Notebooks on Poetry and Politics*. New York: W. W. Norton.

Robertson, J. 1999. "Teaching about Worlds of Hurt through Encounters with Literature: Reflections on Pedagogy." In *Teaching for a Tolerant World, Grades K-6: Essays and Resources* edited by Judith Robertson, 275–93. New York: National Council of English Teachers.

———. 2001. "What Happens to Our Wishes: Magical Thinking in Harry Potter?" *Children's Literature Association Quarterly* 26, no. 4: 198–211.

———, and L. Radford. 2009. "The Private Uses of Quiet Grandeur: A Meditation on Literary Pilgrimage." *Changing English* 16, no. 2: 203–209.

Rose, J. 1984. *The Case of Peter Pan, Or the Impossibility of Children's Fiction.* Philadelphia: University of Pennsylvania Press.

Rousseau, J. J. 1979. *Emile or On Education*. New York: Basic Books.

Rushdie, S. 2005. "The Art of Fiction No. 186." *The Paris Review*, no. 174. Accessed March 14. http://www.theparisreview.com/viewinterview.php/prmMID/5531.

Schlink, B. 1997. *The Reader*. New York: Vintage Books.

Segal, H. 1957. "Notes on Symbol Formation." *International Journal of Psychoanalysis* 38: 391–97.

Self, W. 2014. "The Novel Is Dead. (This Time It's for Real)." *The Guardian Books.* Accessed June 5. http://www.theguardian.com/books/2014/may/02/will-self-novel-dead-literary-fiction.

Sendak, M. 2000. *Where the Wild Things Are*. New York: Red Fox.

Silverstein, S. 1974. *Where the Sidewalk Ends*. New York: Harper Collins.

Simon, R. I. 2005. *The Touch of the Past. Remembrance, Learning, and Ethics.* New York: Palgrave McMillan.

———. 2006. "The Terrible Gift. Museums and the Possibility of Hope without Consolation." *Museum Management and Curatorship* 21, no. 3: 187–204.

Street, B. V. 2005. *Literacies across Educational Contexts: Mediating Learning and Teaching*. Philadelphia: Caslon Publications.

Springgay, S., and D. Freedman, eds. 2012. *Mothering a Bodied Curriculum. Emplacement, Desire, Affect.* Toronto: University of Toronto Press.

Spivak, G. 1976. "Translators Preface." In J. Derrida, *Of Grammatology*. Baltimore: Johns Hopkins University Press.

———. 1988. "Can the Subaltern Speak?" In *Marxism and the Interpretation of Culture*, edited by C. Nelson and L. Grossberg, 271–313. London: MacMillan.

———. 1992. "The Burden of English Studies." In *The Lie of the Land: English Literary Studies in India* edited by R. S. Rajan, 275–99. Delhi: Oxford University Press.

———. 1997. "Teaching for the Times." In *Dangerous Liaisons: Gender, Nations, and Postcolonial Perspectives*, edited by A. McClintock, A. Mufti, and E. Shohat, 468–90. Minneapolis: University of Minnesota Press.

———. 1999. *A Critique of Postcolonial Reason: Toward a History of the Vanishing Present*. Cambridge: Harvard University Press.

———. 2002. "At Both Ends of the Spectrum." Paper presented at the *Living literacies* Conference, Toronto. Accessed May 3. http://www.nald.ca/fulltext/ltonword/part5/spivak/spivak.pdf.

———. 2003. *Death of a Discipline*. New York: Columbia University Press.

———. 2004. "Righting Wrongs." *The South Atlantic Quarterly* 103, no. 2 and 3: 523–81.

Sumara, D. J. 2002. "Creating Commonplaces for Interpretation: Literary Anthropology and Literacy Education Research." *Journal of Literacy Research* 34, no. 2: 237–60.

Tarc, P. 2013. *International Education in Global Times. Engaging the Pedagogic.* New York: Peter Lang.

Torgovnick, M. 1990. *Gone Primitive: Savage Intellects, Modern Lives.* Chicago: University of Chicago Press.

UNESCO. 2000. "The Dakar Framework for Action." In *Education for All: Meeting Our Commitments.* Paris: UNESCO.

Vidal, G. 2008. "Tarzan Revisited." *Esquire.* Accessed May 14. http://www.esquire.com/features/gore-vidal-archive/tarzan-revisited-1263.

Walkerdine, V. 1988. *The Mastery of Reason. Cognitive Development and the Production of Rationality.* London: Routledge.

Webster's Dictionary. 1987. *The New Lexicon Webster's Dictionary of the English Language.* New York: Lexicon Publishers.

Willinsky, J. 1991. *The Triumph of Literature—The Fate of Literacy: English in the Secondary School Curriculum.* New York: Teachers College Press.

———. 1998. *Learning to Divide the World: Education at Empire's End.* Minneapolis: University of Minnesota Press.

Winnicott, D. 1960. "The Theory of the Parent-Child Relationship." *International Journal of Psychoanalysis* 41: 585–95.

Wyatt, J. 1993. "Giving Body to the Word: The Maternal Symbolic in Toni Morrison's *Beloved*." *PMLA* 108, no. 3: 474–88.

Index